CHARACTERISTICS OF A CARING HOME

H. Norman Wright
Rex Johnson

A SUBSIDIARY OF THE BENSON COMPANY
365 Great Circle Road/Nashville, Tennessee 37228

Characteristics Of A Caring Home

Printed in the United States of America.

CONTENTS

Chapters 1-5 by H. Norman Wright
Chapters 6-7 by Rex Johnson

INTRODUCTION

"A Home Full of Christians, or a Christian Home?"

Most sincere Christian married couples would like to establish a *Christian home*. That phrase is tossed around a great deal, but it is seldom defined. As a result, members of the typical Christian family are confused about their goals; they wouldn't know for sure if they really had a Christian home.

Some people would define what a Christian home is so loosely that it would have little meaning. Are we talking about any home in the so-called "Christian nations"—Western Europe and North America? Or are we talking about a home where all the members are Christians, truly born again?

The latter may be described as a *home full of Christians*. It is the point of this book that a *Christian home* is something more than just a *home full of Christians*. It is a family where *relationships are patterned after the way God interacts with His people.*

In order to discover what that model relationship is like, we will study in depth one passage of Scripture. In it the Apostle Paul explains that a believer's relationship with God is based on the fact that he has been *justified* (pronounced Not Guilty) through believing in Jesus Christ. Flowing from that justification, there are several qualities or characteristics of the relationship that exists between God and His people. Here is the passage, with the significant results of justification italicized:

"Therefore, having been justified by faith, *we have peace with God* through our Lord Jesus Christ, through whom also we have obtained our introduction by faith into *this grace in which we stand,* and *we exult in hope* of the glory of God. And not only this, but *we also exult in our tribulations*, knowing that tribulation brings about perseverance, and perseverance, proven character, and proven character, hope. And hope does not disappoint, because *the love of God has been poured out within our hearts through the Holy Spirit* who was given to us. For while we were still helpless, at the right time, Christ died for the ungodly" (Romans 5:1-6).

The word "introduction" (in other translations, "access") is very important. It indicates that we are now allowed to go into God's presence, whereas previously we weren't. We now have the right to enter. Another way of looking at it is that because of Christ we are now fit to enter. We have been changed into the kind of people God likes to have in His presence.

When a person is justified by faith, he has an open relationship with God, and all the results of justification—peace, grace, victory in tribulations, hope, love and the Holy Spirit—are part of his experience. However, he may have all these and *still not be expressing them within his family.* He may have peace with God, yet be at war with other family members. He may have God's love in his heart, but not show it to his wife and children. His may be a *home full of Christians,* but it is not a *Christian home.*

In the following chapters we will examine each of the results of justification to see how it can be applied in your family to create a truly Christian home. We will see that the results of justification experienced by a person who accepts Christ are also the characteristics of a Christian home. This means that our homes will become truly Christian as we allow the eternal life God has already given us to flow throughout our families.

1

PEACE IN THE CHRISTIAN HOME

". . . we have peace with God . . ."

A Home Full of Christians

HAVE PEACE WITH GOD

Our joy and pain are shared with God.

We are subject to God's discipline instead of God's punishment.

Our growing intimacy with God is based on His faithfulness.

A Christian Home

IS A PEACEFUL HOME

Our joy and pain are shared with one another as well.

Mutual accountability is based on discipline instead of punishment.

Growing family intimacy is based on mutual faith in God.

When you and I were justified by faith, God declared an armistice with us, so now there is peace. And as a result, all sorts of communication channels have been opened to us that previously were closed. Our new access to God is expressed in Hebrews 4:16, where we are urged to "draw near with confidence to the throne of grace."

Dr. Martin Lloyd-Jones has written: "When a person has peace with God, the person's mind is at rest about his relationship with God."[1] I don't have to debate anymore whether God has accepted me. I know that He has because of what He has done for me in Christ Jesus; I have that assurance within me. I know that God loves me in spite of my sin. He does not wait until I am perfect. God's love is an unconditional commitment toward imperfect people. I may have doubts, but I can quickly get rid of them when I remind myself of my justification through Christ. God's peace will overcome doubts. This peace with God even conquers the fear of death and of judgment. This implication of peace comes as a process with some people, while others immediately experience it when they accept the Lord. Some only gradually grow into it as their understanding deepens through life experiences.

Recently I heard Dr. Stanley Collins make a very interesting statement: "A Christian does not fear death, but Christians do fear the process of dying." Because we are afraid of that unknown factor, of the pain that could be part of our dying, we are likely to fear the experience. But death itself is not frightening to a believer.

A person who is justified has peace with God. It follows, then, that a truly Christian home will be a peaceful home. Specifically, what does this mean? When you have peace with God, He opens up the communication channels so that you have the opportunity to really share your joy and your pain and your hurts with Him. This kind of intimate sharing will also be characteristic of a truly Christian home.

No Longer God's Enemies

A common false assumption is that God has no enemies except Satan. But John 3:16-21 says:

> For God so loved the world that He gave His only begotten Son that whoever believes in Him should not perish, but have eternal life. For God did not send the Son into the world to judge the world; but that the world should be saved through Him. He who believes in Him is not judged; he who does not believe has been judged already, because he has not believed in the name of the only begotten Son of God. And this is the judgment, that the light is come into the world, and men loved the darkness rather than the light; for their deeds were evil. For everyone who does evil hates the light, and does not come to the light, lest his deeds should be exposed. But he who practices the truth comes to the light, that his deeds may be manifested as having been wrought in God.

So, peace with God is a very important result of justification. It means I'm not an enemy of the God who built the universe.

I've often tried to imagine what it would be like to be on the FBI's most wanted list. Being God's enemy is worse than being wanted dead or alive by not only the FBI, but also the U.S. Army, the city police, the Mafia and, worst of all, the Internal Revenue Service. The only way to cope with the idea of being God's enemy is to deny it. But that doesn't change the fact. It's like telling ourselves we don't have cancer when the doctor says we are full of it. Being justified by God removes the jeopardy, the fear, the awful alienation. We who were His enemies have peace with God instead.

Peace in the Home is not Automatic

Transferring this peace to home relationships is not easy or automatic. I find that there are many Christians who have quite an active prayer life, and they talk very openly about the Lord, yet, unfortunately, they are still strangers, in some respects, to their own family members. I have met women who have said, "The only time I really know what is going on inside of my husband is when he is talking with some business associates in my presence." He never comes right out and shares this information with her.

In contrast to this, one characteristic of a Christian home is that our joy and our pain are shared with one another. When you share your joy with another person or another group of individuals, that joy actually spreads. It is infectious, spreading from one person to another, and they are able to be joyful with you. In Romans 12:13 we read that we are to "rejoice with those who rejoice" and to "weep with those who weep." In Galatians 6:2 we are told that we are to "bear one another's burdens," but how in the world are we to bear another's burdens unless that person is willing to share the burden with us? In some cases we expect our family members to be mind-readers and to know automatically when we are happy and delighted and when we're hurting.

Perhaps you have had the experience in which one of your children has come home with his or her face covered with a gloomy mask. You say, "What's wrong?" and the answer is, "Nothing, nothing's wrong." At the same time you're getting a different message because their "non-verbal" communication is saying that something is wrong. It is at times like this that we as parents must have quite a bit of patience and listening ability. We need to make ourselves available so that eventually the child will have the freedom to open up and share this hurt with us. This is one way that we can be a support system.

There are even churches where members sit side by side sharing their joys and their hurts with the Lord, but they don't feel free to turn to the person next to them and say, "I'd like you to pray for me, because this is what's going on in my life," or "Can I tell you the exciting thing that happened to me last week?" We carry this same isolation into our homes. Our children may come home and share an experience that is a delight to them. But perhaps there is one small element in what they are sharing with us that we don't care for or we don't exactly agree with. Instead of just responding by sharing in their joy, we enter into the "parent" role and become the critic. We focus on that one small area because we are so certain that they're not aware of it. We want to correct it. When I find myself doing this, I try to tell myself, "Be quiet and enter into the joy that is there."

Sharing Our Hurts Builds Family Peace

I remember a very vivid experience that I had with my daughter Sheryl. We have a game at home that we like to play now and then, called the "Ungame." One time my daughter and I were playing it, and she drew a card which said: "Jesus wept. What do you sometimes feel like crying about? Have you ever asked a family member that question? Do you know what they would say?"

When Sheryl answered, we put the game away, and she and I talked for fifteen minutes. I was beginning to hear about some things that were going on inside of her. Then I had the opportunity as the father, the "strong one," to share some hurts in my life. That one fifteen-minute experience drew us much closer together because a deeper understanding came from a greater bearing of one another's burdens. One of the insights which came out of that conversation was that Sheryl had some very strong feelings about Matthew, her brother, who is retarded. We were assuming that she was handling the situation sufficiently, but she wasn't. Some of her questions, and her fears began to come out in that little time of sharing.

One crucial experience that has helped me begin to share my feelings, my hurts and my joys was the discovery that our son was retarded. We first knew something was wrong when he began having grand mal seizures, which are very frightening to a person who has never seen one before, especially when they're being suffered by a family member. For a period of about three months, the doctors couldn't discover what the problem was. I was around home much of the time, because it was summer and I was working on a book, and I got the strong impression that my wife Joyce was holding in a few more of her feelings than usual. I could see through her non-verbal responses our son's problem was weighing a great deal upon her. I wished I could reach inside of her, take out that pain and carry it around so that she didn't have to experience it. Week after week I felt that way, but I never told her until months later. When I finally did share this with her, she started crying and said, "I wish you had shared that with me before, because it would have helped me so much in getting through the summer." I was expecting Joyce to be a mind-reader, which is totally unfair. How was she to know what I was feeling? I had a feeling of care and compassion, but I failed to express it. How can our families be loving support systems unless we can move into one another's lives and talk in this intimate way.

Discipline is Different from Punishment

There is another aspect of our peace with God. Because we are at peace with God, we are now subject to His discipline instead of His punishment. Peace with God really removes us from the threat of God's vengeance. We read in John 3:18, "He who believes in Him is not judged; he who does not believe has been judged already." Instead of punishing us, God disciplines us. We see this in Hebrews 12:5-11:

> And you have forgotten the exhortation which is addressed to you as sons, "My son, do not regard lightly the discipline of the Lord, nor faint when you are reproved by

Him, for those whom the Lord loves He disciplines and He scourges every son whom He receives." It is for discipline that you endure; God deals with you as with sons, for what son is there whom his father does not discipline? But, if you are without discipline, of which all have become partakers, then you are illegitimate children and not sons. Furthermore, we had earthly fathers to discipline us, and we respected them; shall we not much rather be subject to the Father of spirits and live? For they disciplined us for a short time as seemed best to them, but He disciplines us for our good, that we may share His holiness. All discipline for the moment seems not to be joyful, but sorrowful; yet to those who have been trained by it, afterwards it yields the peaceful fruit of righteousness.

This truth can be easily related to a home context. We are suggesting here that because of justification we are subject to God's discipline instead of His punishment. When we transfer this principle to the Christian home, we see that there is mutual accountability between family members, based on discipline rather than punishment. I see families where the dominant characteristic of their home is punishment. And often the punishment is very extreme.

Unfortunately, there is a lot of confusion over the difference between discipline and punishment. I'm grateful to Bruce Narramore and his book, *Help! I'm a Parent!* for the distinction between punishment and discipline:[2]

	Punishment	Discipline
Purpose	To inflict penalty for an offense	To train for correction and maturity
Focus	Past misdeeds	Future correct acts
Attitude	Hostility and frustration on the part of the parent	Love and concern on the part of the parent
Resulting emotion in the child	Fear and guilt	Security

The purpose of punishment is to inflict penalty for an offense, but the purpose of discipline is to train for correction and maturity. The word "discipline" has the same root meaning as the word "disciples." The disciples were learners. One essential aspect of discipline is teaching.

The focus of punishment is on past wrong deeds; the focus in discipline is on future correct deeds. It's so easy, especially for parents, bosses and teachers to respond only to past misdeeds and go over and over what people have done wrong. The only difficulty is that if we spend 90 percent of our time going over what they have done wrong, then we can spend only 10 percent of our time trying to help them to do the correct things in the future. We are actually paying more attention to what they have done wrong and therefore are reinforcing their wrong behavior. It is far better to spend less time on what a person has done wrong and spend more time talking about what it is that we would like to see them do.

A Negative Spirit Destroys Peace

If you have a complaint against a family member, for example, you probably share it in a very general, negative way: "You're never affectionate." "You don't communicate with me." Now, what does "affectionate" mean? What does "communicate" mean? The person you're complaining to hasn't got much to go on if he wants to correct his behavior. There are going to be some legitimate complaints within our families. But instead of allowing your complaints to be negative and general, make them specific and positive.

A man came in for counseling and said: "My wife complained to me that I'm never affectionate. Well, I don't know what that means. Am I supposed to hold her hand, kiss her, and say 'hello'? What am I supposed to do?" As we worked together he gained some new insight into what his wife really meant. She, on her part, agreed to be more specific. The way in which she learned to approach him was to say something like, "Honey, I would appreciate it if you would greet me with a kiss when you come home from work each day." "I would appreciate it if you would let me know when you like a meal." Or, "If we're out in public, I would really appreciate it if you would hold my hand." Now, those specific complaints gave her husband definite goals to work toward.

When your child misbehaves, what do you say? "You are a sloppy mess! Look at this house!" Well, you know, that might be true, but does it bring about the change that you desire? Instead say, "Hey, I would really appreciate it if you would take about ten minutes right now and go through your room, make up your bed, hang up the clothes. . . ." If we just out-line what we want done, and we say it in a proper tone of voice, we may see a better response.

Whenever another person has done something right, whether it is an employee, a fellow worker, a person you are serving with on the board at church, or a family member, let him know that you appreciate it. Encourage him, reinforce him. Do not take people for granted. First Thessalonians 5:11 tells us to "En-courage one another." I have met some parents who say, "I don't dare tell my child he has done a good job, because then he will slack off." You know, after a while, that child will become so discouraged that he's going to say, "Why bother? It's never recognized." I've also met some husbands who say, "Why should I thank my wife for always having my clothes clean or for cooking the dinner? That's her job, isn't it?" Perhaps that is something that she has been assigned to do, but it is still an act of love toward her husband. I think if we husbands would approach it in that way, our wives would feel better about their work. We all need encouragement, but we take one another for granted.

Make Sure Discipline Has a Constructive Purpose

As you think of discipline's focus on future correct deeds, consider this suggestion: If you are a parent disciplining your children, ask yourself the question, "Why? What is my purpose in discipline? What is it that I would like my children to become? What is my goal for my child, for my adolescent, or even the goal that I would like to see my spouse or mother-in-law work toward?" You see, we would like people to change, but we have given little thought to the end product we desire. What about letting the fruit of the Spirit of Galatians 5:22-23 be the goal toward which we would want to encourage our family members to move? Then the guiding principle in our discipline will be: How should we behave in order to encourage other people to move toward the fruits of the Spirit in their lives?

There is a contrast in the attitudes with which punishment and discipline are administered. The attitude in punishment is usually hostility and frustration on the part of the parent. We're reacting because we've been thwarted and frustrated. But discipline is done out of love and concern on the part of the parent. This is not always obvious to the child, and even the parent may feel a mixture of motives. The general rule of thumb ought to be: Deal with your anger and frustration first, then with your child. It may take several days, but eventually we can come to the place where we can very calmly say, "You know, Johnny, this is what happened the other day, and I would really like to talk to you about it because it really bothered me." It might take several days of rehearsing it in my mind to be able to say it in such a calm fashion, but I will get a much better response if I do.

Positive Discipline Will Have a Positive Response

The resulting emotions a child feels when you punish him are usually fear and guilt. But when there is discipline, the child feels secure. I have heard a number of children say: "You know, my parents are stricter with me than other parents are with their kids, but that's all right, because I know they care for me, and I feel O.K. about it. I know when I blow it; I know when I do something wrong. And I know they have to do this."

Recently I had an unusual experience. I was preparing a tape on discipline, and instead of simply lecturing I decided to sit down with my daughter and tape a two-way conversation between us about discipline. Being in high school, she's been through many stages of the process of discipline. I decided to ask her questions and get her ideas. At one point in the conversation I shared with her the punishment/discipline diagram and discussed it. When I got to the part where it stated the resulting emotion in the child—with punishment "the child feels fear and guilt," but with discipline, "he feels secure,"—I asked, "What do you think about that?" And one of her responses was, "Well, the fear is not so much for the punishment. I guess, the fear comes from the way in which the parent is talking. If the parent would talk in a normal voice, without that intense tone, or raising the voice, I think there would be less fear." I think there is a great deal of validity to that.

So, as you can see, there are a lot of differences between punishment and discipline. God disciplines His children; He doesn't punish us. This is the model for us as parents. As we become more in tune with the way God interacts with us, we'll interact with our children in a more constructive way, and less on the basis of our emotional reactions.

Submissive Authority

Understanding what God has done for us in justification will give us a new basis for discipline, too.

The old basis, the world's basis, is power. That was true in Jesus' day and it's true today. Roman military power was absolute, and its philosophy permeated not only the government but also business, athletics and even family roles. Our world today is still dependent on lines of authority based on power. This is true in government, business, and even in family relationships. That's why families experience power struggles—between husbands and wives, between parents and children, and among children. But Jesus' way of interacting contrasts sharply with society's. As Philippians 2:5-8 shows, Jesus *gave up* power:

> —Jesus was born in a manger, not a palace.
>
> —He grew up as a Palestinian carpenter, not a Roman dignitary.
>
> —In His own words, he came to serve, not to be served.
>
> —Even after dying on a cross as a sacrifice for sin, He served breakfast on the beach to His disciples after His resurrection.

Servanthood is the basis for relationships among God's people. Ephesians 5:21 puts it this way: "Be subject to one another in the fear of Christ." Romans 15:1-13 exhorts us to servant roles and shows us how and why. The whole New Testament is written from this perspective. The servant role is the basis for discipline in the church. Matthew 18:15-17 teaches that we are the servants of our brothers even when they sin.

Notice that the basis for discipline in the church is *mutual accountability*, not some sort of court or power system. In my family, if mutual accountability is the basis for discipline several good things happen:

1. There are fewer and fewer power struggles.

2. There is less tendency to punish, more of a tendency to discipline.

3. As family leader my authority can be based on service instead of power.

4. As I initiate accountability to family members, they tend to reciprocate, thereby learning responsibility and self-discipline.

5. Our interactions are "Christian" in contrast to the power-based interactions of our culture.

Here's how we can establish mutual accountability:

1. Each family member accepts the role of servant to the rest of the family.

2. The family leader needs to share an area in his life in which he wants to grow and volunteer accountability to the family for growth in that area. That means that when he doesn't grow or when he makes mistakes or fails in the area that he has made himself accountable to his family, they are to mention it to him to help him grow.

3. Over time, as the person or persons who initiate servanthood and accountability change and grow, the rest of the family will reciprocate and mutual accountability will grow.

Growing in Intimacy

A further aspect of the peace that comes from

justification is that we have a growing intimacy with God which is based on His faithfulness. What do you think of when you hear the word "intimate"? Webster's dictionary defines it as "most private or personal, very close and familiar, deep and thorough."[3] For intimacy to exist, there must be trust, because sharing personal aspects of our lives makes us vulnerable. As we trust God we begin to learn how great is His faithfulness. We can trust Him more and more and open up more and more of our selves to Him.

In a Christian home, we also can have a growing *family* intimacy. For this to happen we need to trust each other, but as Christians our family intimacy can be based on mutual faith in God. Now, again, many people have this intimacy in their relationship with God, but intimacy toward family members has never been developed. Believers have the greatest opportunity of being able to develop an intimacy with their families because of the pattern of intimacy that is experienced with the Lord.

To better understand what we mean by intimacy, let's turn to a popular analysis of communication as an illustration. This particular outline has been developed by John Powell as an explanation of different levels of interpersonal communication:[4]

Level five is communicating by exchanging cliches. "How are you doing? How's your dog? How's your wife? New car you've got there." We just spout these things off; they really don't have that much meaning. Some are said just to be polite or to fill an embarrassing silence. Often when you get off the airplane you can predict exactly what the stewardess is going to say. It's part of the routine; it's part of the job. It doesn't have too much meaning. Unfortunately, in many homes the family members don't communicate any more deeply than on the cliche level. I have encountered some families where a man is hardly given a warm greeting when he comes home at night. In return, he gives the dog more attention than he gives his wife. You can live together in a home and still be strangers because you are limited to cliche communication.

Maybe one reason why our family communication is on the cliche level is that our conversation with God is just that superficial. What is your prayer life like? Do you simply throw a series of cliches toward God? Would my prayer this morning be identical with one I offered six months ago? Listen to your prayer at the dinner table. Listen to your family prayers. Are they monotonously the same? Is there meaning, or are you just spouting words that really have no depth of meaning?

One way to test your family communication level is to think back to last year and what you were talking about. Compare that with what you are talking about this year. Is it basically the same content? Maybe some different issues have come up now, but are they in reality the same subjects? Another way to test for cliches is to list what you've talked about as a family during the last week. Is the list predictable for next week, too? If it is, chances are you're stuck with cliches.

Level four communication is the reporting of facts. We're like newspaper reporters. We don't have any personal investment in the conversation. We don't show our feelings, we don't reveal our thoughts; we just rattle off the facts. We still do not experience any real intimacy or closeness.

Our prayer life may also be stuck on level four.

"Lord, bless the missionaries; help them to do this; help our church to do this." We go through the routine, but the feeling is not there. We don't share genuine concern: "I'm really upset about some things that have been happening in my life lately."

The Deeper Levels of Intimacy

Getting below level four is less common than most people realize. Try a conversation sometime without talking about your job, other people, your children, or sports. Or, to help get on to level three, try playing The Ungame for a while and notice how it helps you all express yourselves at level three. Any of the decks will do. They will help you talk about your values, your beliefs, your thoughts, your ideas. If playing The Ungame is a refreshing change, play it often.

Level three would involve a sharing of our ideas and judgments. "This is what I think about what's going on at work." "You know what I learned today in Bible study fellowship?—let me share it with you." We hope the other person is tuned in as we begin to share things that are important to us. When we get to this level, we have just begun to communicate. At level three we can have disagreements and arguments, and we can challenge one another. If we're mature, we can even allow the other person to think differently from us and disagree with us. In fact a mature person encourages his family to form their own judgments and ideas even if they are different from his.

But *level two* goes even deeper. The real intimacy in any relationship begins to develop when two people begin to share their innermost feelings, their emotions, and there's a power and depth behind their sharing. Each person involved must first be *mutually accessible*. Each has free access to the other person without fear of criticism or restraint. It means a trust and honesty in the relationship and it is mutual. To develop intimacy we need to open our lives and allow ourselves to be known by other people. This is risky because it opens the door for rejection. But you also open the door for a deeper relationship.

Jesus Himself was open and vulnerable. He was sensitive to others' feelings. When He came upon Mary and Martha hurting because of Lazarus' death, He wept with them. The Jewish people thought He was weeping because of His love for Lazarus. But within that love Jesus was probably moved by compassion because of His sensitivity to the pain of the loss of Mary and Martha. When you let a family member venture into your world of feelings you then begin to develop true intimacy.

Apply this principle to your prayer life. Can you remember the last time when you "agonized" in prayer? When there was so much tremendous feeling behind it that you were almost crying out to the Lord? Unfortunately, it often takes a crisis for us to do this.

I was driving home from Biola College one day, and I was stopped at a railroad intersection. I could observe that there was a freight train stopped about a hundred feet away from the crossing to drop a car. Automobiles were lined up each way, and I gathered they had been waiting for a while. Some began to drive around the crossing gate out of impatience. But I could see what they couldn't. There was an Amtrak passenger train coming up the track. I sat there and watched a tragedy unfold. A VW Rabbit started to creep across the tracks. I saw the engineer of the freight train try to wave the person back, and then I saw him turn around and walk away as though he didn't want to look at what was going to happen. I heard the train whistle, and then I saw it hit that car broadside. The VW flew into the air, almost totally demolished, and fell to the ground.

The frustration of seeing this was overwhelming. I knew it was going to happen and I couldn't do anything about it. A flood of emotion hit me. Helpless, I pulled out of line, found a phone, called for the paramedics and the fire department and left for home.

Anyone nearby would have thought I was crazy. I was driving with my eyes open, but I was talking out loud. I was praying with more feeling than I had prayed for months, saying, "Lord, you know if the person is still alive. If they are not a Christian, save them." I prayed that they were Christians. I prayed for someone to help them. I prayed for the family. I prayed all the way home.

This was during the time when my daughter was taking driver's training, and as I drove up, she was getting into the car. I couldn't help reflecting back to what had happened. As I walked into the house, my wife walked by, and I didn't even say hello at this time. I said "Sheryl is not driving today." They said, "What's wrong?" and I said, "I think I just saw a person killed in an accident." I walked into the other end of the house with Joyce following me, and then I just let loose. I got out my anger, my frustration, my hurt. I was talking, I was crying and walking around. Joyce didn't know exactly what to do; she just stood there. That was fine, because it was consoling enough so that I could share and talk with her to get the feelings out of my system. But why does it take events like that to deepen our prayer life?

Well, let me tell you the outcome, because God works in so many miraculous ways. Three cars from the VW was a young girl from Biola College who had not wanted to take the anatomy course which she had just finished. She got out of her car, rushed to the wreckage, put on three tourniquets and saved the life of the girl who was driving. That girl today is almost perfectly well. She's a violinist, and her fingers are just about back to where she can play.

People have said, "You know, it sounds like a miracle that she's alive." All I can say is that if you had been there and had seen that accident, you would have known that God had His hand in it to preserve her life, because no one could have lived through that otherwise.

Could it be that there is something that we should deal with in our life that might compel us to pray in this way? Or maybe there's no great crisis; we just need to get down and say, "God, I want to tell you what's going on in my life. I have feelings of joy, and I want to share them with you. And I'm a little upset at times at work, and I'd like to share that with you, too."

Level One Communication

Now, the deepest level of communication is what Powell calls *Level one*. It's hard to explain. It is a "peak communication" when two of you are really relating to one another in many dimensions, feelings, thoughts, ideas. When you come away from such an experience, you know that you've really had an intensely wonderful communications experience. Level one communication is rare, as John Powell is quick to point out. But it can happen. I remember occasions when in my prayer time I have sensed the presence of the Lord there in a striking way. I just opened up, and I knew that I was being taken in and He was responding. There are many other times when I don't have that feeling. But to have any kind of intimacy, this is the kind of communication that we need to work toward. We may be afraid to open up, but our fears will disappear when we realize that He already sees us as we are, and yet He values us as so worthwhile and adequate that He sent His Son, Jesus Christ, to die for us. If we realize that we have that much value and worth to God, then we can experience a new freedom in prayer and can really pour out our hearts to Him. This in turn will enable us to be free to share on a more intimate level with our families, so that our homes can begin taking steps toward being what can be truly called Christian homes, instead of just homes full of Christians.

FOOTNOTES

[1]Martin Lloyd-Jones, *Spiritual Depression* (Grand Rapids, MI: W. B. Eerdmans, 1965), adapted from chapter 19.
[2]Bruce Narramore, *Help! I'm a Parent* (Grand Rapids, MI: Zondervan, 1975), page 41.
[3]*Webster's Seventh New Collegiate Dictionary* (Springfield, MO: G. & C. Merriam Co., 1966), page 444.
[4]John Powell, *Why Am I Afraid to Tell You Who I Am?* (Niles, IL: Argus Communications, 1969), pages 54-62.

GRACE IN THE CHRISTIAN HOME

". . . this grace in which we stand . . ."

A Home Full of Christians
STAND IN GRACE

God forgave all our sins; Jesus took the blame.

God does not reject or condemn us when we sin.

God grants us the status of co-heirs with Christ.

A Christian Home
IS A GRACIOUS HOME

We don't have to cast blame in family conflict—Jesus took it.

We can accept one another even when we disapprove of behavior.

Is characterized by respect and enabling rather than intra-family competition.

The basic distinction that we are making in applying the results of justification listed in Romans 5:1-6 is that between a home full of Christians and a

Christian home. It's not that one is bad and the other is good, but that one is good and the other is much better. The key question is this: Are our homes really benefiting from what God has done in our individual lives? We might have a very close relationship with Him, but the presence of Jesus Christ in our lives may not greatly affect the way we relate to one another in our home situation.

What Is This Thing Called Grace?

The second result of justification is *grace*. The idea of standing in grace means that God has forgiven all of our sins because Jesus has taken the blame for them. Now, the word "grace" is a very, very important word for the Christian life. It is defined as "unmerited favor," and it is also called "God's gift" (Romans 3:24). The benefits of grace always go to the undeserving person. God is saying, "Here it is, regardless of whether you deserve it or not." In Ephesians 2:8 we read that it is by His grace that we are saved from the consequences of sin. One of the main truths behind our "standing in grace" is that God declares us to be righteous, not because of anything that we have done, but because Jesus took the blame for our sin.

In his book *Free for the Taking*, Joseph Cooke shares the following:

> This, then, is the wonder of the Christian message, that God is this kind of God, that He loves me, and is not "turned off" by my sins, my failures, my inadequacies, my insignificance. I am not a stranger in a

terrifying universe. I am not a disease crawling on the face of an insignificant speck in the vast emptiness of space. I am not a nameless insect waiting to be crushed by an impersonal boot. I am not a miserable offender cowering under the glare of an angry deity. I am a man, beloved by God, Himself. I have touched the very heart of the universe and found His name to be Love. And that love has reached me, not because I have merited God's favor, not because I have anything to boast about, but because of what He is, and because of what Christ has done for me in the Father's name. And I can believe this about God, and therefore, about myself, because Christ has come from the Father and is revealed by His teaching, by His life, by His death, by His very person that this is what God is like, He is full of grace.[1]

God doesn't blame us any more for our sins, because Jesus has taken our blame. It may be said that God is very, very gracious toward each one of us. The word, "gracious" means: accepting, kind, courteous, pleasing, merciful.

Grace in the Christian Home

It's one thing to realize and be thankful for what God has done for us, but it is something else to turn this into a model of how we respond to one another within the context of our family. Here we will see a clearcut difference between a home full of Christians and a Christian home. In a Christian home, we don't feel the need to cast blame upon other people in family conflict, because Jesus has taken care of the blame. Many times we try to resolve differences within the home by pointing the finger at someone else and saying, "You are the one who is responsible." We feel that by finding someone to blame we have solved the problem.

The Atmosphere in a Legalistic Home

Such homes are dominated by a spirit of legalism, rather than by a gracious type of atmosphere. In a legalistic type of a home, you would probably find someone who actually feels like a worm, because of the comments made toward him or her. There is constant condemnation and blame.

Another characteristic of a legalistic home is the tendency to constantly ask the question, "All right, who did it?" I have caught myself automatically responding in this way. I'll misplace my pen or my glasses case, and then I'll walk in where Joyce and Sheryl are and say, "O.K., who did it? Which one of you guys took it? I know that one of you picked it up and put it some place, and I just can't find it." What is really embarrassing is if one of them just reaches in my pocket and pulls out the pen!

Have you found yourself asking the question, "Who did it?" in your home? Then think about this: "Why is it important that I find that someone else was responsible? Couldn't it have been me? Or, does it really matter? Is that really a crucial issue for the health and the welfare of my family?" In many cases, it isn't.

How Legalistic Relationships Are Balanced

One of the reasons that blaming and its opposite, placating, are so prevalent in families is that blaming and placating are used to restore balance in relationships in a home. You see, many homes are built on the principle of balanced relationships. Picture a teeter-totter. A bride and groom stand close together at the center, the fulcrum. It is in balance. Now one of them may mistake something the other said, or may forget something, or may be rude in some way. The other person gets the feeling that he or she isn't important enough to the spouse. This person feels like the relationship is now out of balance, so he or she responds with a comment that is intended to lower the spouse's self-esteem and restore balance. It is as if one spouse moved a step away from the fulcrum, and the teeter-totter became uneven. The other spouse's response is to move a step away from the fulcrum on his or her side to bring the teeter-totter back to a horizontal position. The relationship, like the teeter-totter, is back in balance now, but the couple are two steps apart. This kind of constant rebalancing of the relationship often continues until the husband and wife are poised on either end of the relationship ready to jump off! As a couple step away from each other in their relationship, trying to regain balance, they often use blame as a way to avoid responsibility for the alienation. Blaming the other person is their way of tolerating the relationship until balance is restored.

Another characteristic of a legalistic home is wh we call "nagging." We're constantly on the other son's case, going over and over and over their with a critical tone to our voice. We justify thi idea that we're trying to motivate him to change for his own good.

Now, let me clarify something. Nagging is not the same as reminding. Many people confuse these. Nagging is a negative, critical, fault-finding, persistent harping, in which the person toward whom it is directed feels very, very irritated. Now, you might be irritated when you are reminded: "I don't like being reminded." Then ask yourself, "Was there ever a time when I gave an indication that I was going to do this thing that they are reminding me about?" If you did give an earlier indication, then the best way to be sure your spouse, parent, or child won't bother you with reminders is to follow through with your commitment before they have to remind you.

Another characteristic of a legalistic home, unfortunately, is that God is presented as a policeman or as a tyrant. A young girl that I worked with many years ago came out of a home in which the way in which the mother (who, unfortunately, was mentally ill) told her what she wanted done was to say, "The Lord has given me another vision of what you are to do tomorrow." If the girl (then about six or seven) would violate what the mother had said, she would also be made to feel she was going against God. Later, when the girl reached the age of eighteen or twenty, one of the struggles that she had to go through was to rid her life of the distorted concept of God that her mother had built. She began a search for who God really is as proclaimed by the Word of God.

Grace Overcomes the Tendency to Blame and Criticize

Instead of looking for others to blame for our home

tensions, let's see how *we* could act in a much more gracious manner. One helpful growth exercise is to ask, "How do I accept just criticism when it comes in my direction?" You see, the word "gracious" means the same thing in human relations as it does when used of God: accepting, kind, courteous, pleasing, merciful. Are we extremely defensive, and do we react to criticism by pointing out the failures in others' lives? Or do we listen carefully to what they're saying and weigh it to see whether there is validity to what they are saying?

The Word of God actually gives us a pattern for how we can respond to criticism. In Proverbs 13:18 we read, "If you refuse criticism, you will end up in poverty and disgrace. If you accept criticism, you are on the road to fame" (These quotes are all from *The Living Bible* translation). Proverbs 23:12—"Don't refuse to accept criticism; get all the help you can." Proverbs 25:12—"It is a badge of honor to accept valid criticism."

Now, I've had people ask the question, "Well, what if the criticism is not valid?" Well, when we are criticized our immediate reaction is usually, "They're wrong! It's not valid." What would happen if we were to take the other position and say, "Maybe it *is* valid," and work from that premise. We might learn a great deal more, and we would certainly overcome some of that spontaneous defensiveness that many of us struggle with. In Proverbs 28:13 we read this: "A man who refuses to admit his mistakes can never be successful; but if he confesses and forsakes them, he gets another chance."

You see, one of the ways in which you can be a gracious person is to respond to the suggestions or criticisms that another person might have for you. As parents in particular, we ought to be concerned about the model we provide for our children in responding to criticism. If I'm concerned because my own daughter has a tendency to be defensive, maybe it is because she has had a model of this from me. Unfortunately, we parents are often excellent teachers in areas where we would prefer not to teach our children. Maybe we will have to go to them and say, "You know, I have not been doing what I would really like to be doing. I'm not really demonstrating the kind of attitude that the Word of God says I should. I'd like to apologize for that, and I am going to be trying to put this into practice in my life." We may think, "Boy! that's hard to say!" Yes, it is hard to say, but its results will make it all worthwhile, for your home will be full of a new gracious atmosphere.

"Love Forgets Mistakes"

A gracious spirit is also essential if we are going to *give* criticism or share complaints with others. How do we do it? Well, the first question is, does it need to be shared? Is it really that vital to the health of the family? In Romans 14:13, we are told: "Stop being so critical of one another. If you must be critical, be critical of yourself, and see that you don't do anything to cause your brother to stumble" (Phillip's translation). And Proverbs 17:9—"Love forgets mistakes, but harping or nagging about them parts even the best of friends." Those three little words are important: "Love forgets mistakes." If a child has done something wrong and we've gone through the process of sharing what it is that we want him to do right, and then say that it's over with, "I've forgiven you," but we constantly bring it up and throw it back at him, we have not really shown love or forgiveness.

Now, to say that we don't have to fix blame among family members does not mean there never will be family conflict. There can be differences and disagreements without the casting of blame. Of course there is going to be conflict within a family, but how we approach and attempt to deal with the conflict is very important. If we are constantly trying to pin the blame on one another, we are not really exercising a life of peace with one another or demonstrating a gracious attitude within our home.

Understanding Family Conflict

Let me share with you six principles concerning conflict in our relationships. First of all, conflict is a natural phenomenon and it is inevitable in our lives. The Scripture does not teach that you will always have a calm and tranquil life just because you are a Christian. You will definitely experience conflict in your family relationships, so just accept that fact.

Second, conflict usually involves personal values and needs. The reason the conflict arises is because there are two sets of values confronting one another; there are two sets of needs coming against one another.

Third, in many cases conflicts emerge as a symptom of a more basic problem. An example of that might be a teenager who causes conflict by asking for a greater latitude in the use of the car and the hour of curfew, while the deeper issue is the need for greater freedom and independence which he is experiencing as a very natural process during his teen years. So when a conflict comes up, instead of always reacting to it at face value, we need to try to discover what is really behind it.

What Causes Anger?

Anger, for instance, is really more of a symptom than the actual problem. There are three common causes for anger. The first is fear. A person experiences some type of a fear in his life, and instead of expressing it as fear, he reacts with anger. A parent may be sitting up at night waiting for his teenager to come in. First he's a half-hour late, and then an hour late. The fear response gradually begins to turn into "Why isn't that kid home?" Then to "Wait until he gets home!" The result is that instead of showing concern and relief and love when the teenager finally walks in, the parent dumps all his pent up anger.

Another reason that we become angry is that we're frustrated because we're not getting our way. And then the third common reason is that we've been hurt in some way.

When I am counseling a client who is extremely angry and hostile, I let them pour out their feelings. But after they have done this and are a little more reasonable, I say: "I'd like to ask you three questions: Is there something that you're afraid of in your life at the present time? Are you experiencing some kind of hurt? Or, is there something that is really frustrating you?" Often it's just like seeing a balloon burst. All the leftover anger begins to dissipate. Then the person may say, "No one has ever asked those questions before, but one of them is right on the button."

I wonder what would happen in your family if,

when a person is angry, you could avoid responding with your own anger, and instead begin talking about him, about his fears, frustrations and hurts. That might show that you have a much greater sensitivity to his needs at this particular moment.

A fourth principle about conflict is that most conflict is not dealt with openly because most people have not been taught effective ways of resolving their feelings. As a result they try to run from conflict situations by whatever method they can come up with. This avoids problems, but does not solve them.

A fifth principle is that conflict provides opportunity for growth in a relationship. Now, you might not believe that at the time when you are experiencing the conflict because some pain might be involved, but conflict is often essential to growth.

The sixth principle is that unresolved conflicts interfere with growth and satisfying relationships. If you would like a different type of a Bible study, let me make a suggestion. Read through the life of Christ in the four Gospels and notice the many occasions in which He was in conflict with other people. Then study His way of resolving these conflicts. He set the example for a very healthy pattern.

How Conflicts Can Be Dealt With

In general, there are five recognizable styles of resolving conflict. People tend to choose one or another of these as a matter of habit. The first style is *withdrawal*. This is a very common pattern. It is used by a person who just can't stand the pain of having differences of opinion. He feels that the best way to have peace and a happy family is not to get involved in the conflict. He just gives up and refuses to discuss the issue. The price he pays is that he doesn't get any of his needs met, and he doesn't get to share his opinions.

On the opposite extreme is the *competitive* style of the person who has to win no matter what. And they can't allow themselves to be on the losing side of an argument, because they don't have a feeling of personal security. They have to maintain control, and always seem to be involved in a power struggle.

A third style is to maintain the conflict for a while, then to *yield*. In this way the person feels, "I'm probably the most gracious one here because I'm always the one who is giving in, while my partner always gets his way."

A fourth style is *compromise*. This is a situation in which both parties give a little and take a little.

But there is still a fifth and better style —*resolution* of the conflict.

Each of these basic styles has certain predictable results. A person who follows a withdrawal pattern finds that he does not build deep relationships, because that type of behavior really does not develop or improve communication between two people, nor does it lead to the achievement of needs. No one who constantly withdraws will find his needs being met. Unfortunately, there are some today who have misinterpreted what the Word of God says about submission, encouraging a kind of withdrawal. People who follow this teaching never fully resolve conflicts.

What about the competitive style that is bent on winning? Winning might get your immediate needs met, but it doesn't do too much for the relationship. If you have to be on top constantly, you don't have much of a concern for the needs of the other person.

Your major concern is yourself and the achievement of your needs.

A yielding style does show a concern for the relationship, but the one who yields is still left frustrated. His needs still are not being met.

The style of compromise falls somewhere between fully meeting your personal needs and concern for the relationship. It isn't always the best way, but it usually helps. Sometimes we will use all of these methods to some extent.

The best method of dealing with conflict, the style that enables you to meet your needs and still shows a high concern for the relationship is the resolution of the conflict so that it is no longer a source of irritation. The problem is that when you bury a conflict, you bury it alive. It hasn't died. It's still living, and growing, and taking new and different shapes.

I believe that one of the ways that we demonstrate grace in our relationships and show that we are gracious individuals is to have the courage to share honestly with another person what the conflict means to us and how we think it should be resolved. This can only be done through prayer and with a great deal of mental rehearsing of what we want to say. Usually, we will have to come up with several alternatives before we find one that is an acceptable resolution for both parties. One of the important elements of this process is to be, as the Scripture says in James 1:19, "a ready listener." We need to listen carefully to the other person, and then, with a proper tone of voice, and having thought it out, share some possibilities and some alternatives.

Be Quick to Forgive

There is a further application of grace in the Christian home. It has to do with the forgiveness of sin. In our relationship with God our sins are forgiven because Christ has carried them for us. Therefore, we are able to confess our sins to Him and be confident of forgiveness.

The same ought to be true in the Christian home. Family members should not go around pointing out one another's sins. Because of our sinful human nature it is easy to fall into the pattern of constantly either being defensive or casting the blame on the other person. Many of us have learned this habit-pattern over many years, so it will take a lot of effort to change it. Grace will begin to operate in our families when we are more anxious to forgive than to find fault with one another.

Often, the reason why we are defensive or cast blame is because of the sinful thoughts in our own mind. So many of our feelings and so much of our behavior comes from what we think about. There is a passage in Proverbs that says, "As a man thinks in his heart, so is he" (Proverbs 23:7). A person who has a tendency toward sinful thoughts may be helped by reading Rom. 12:2; Eph. 4:23; Phil. 4:6-9; I Peter 1:13; Isaiah 26:3.

A further aspect of standing in grace, and building a gracious home, is to try to emulate the fact that God does not reject or condemn us when we sin. How miserable we would be if God had no mercy! If God were a strict disciplinarian, without grace, being a Christian would be a miserable experience. God would be zapping me every day! When we sin we do damage to our fellowship with God. But God doesn't reject or condemn us. He continues to love, and to accept, and to forgive us.

Similarly, in a truly Christian home, we can accept one another even when we disapprove of each other's behavior. When you and I sin, we don't have to work to get back into God's favor. We already stand in grace, which is unmerited favor. The same ought to be true in our families. If unmerited favor is the standing enjoyed by every member, forgiveness will be automatic and the restoration of fellowship will be natural.

Ought-dominated and Fear-dominated Families

We have mentioned the balanced relationship some families set up. Other families establish their relationship on the basis of *oughts*. These homes have an overabundance of oughts. You ought to do this, you ought to do that. They have rules and regulations for everything. In an "ought home," people are pressured to live up to very high standards. When a family member fails to live up to one of them, others in the family will find ways of making him or her feel like a blob! For instance, a person may be called names, like "stupid" and "dummy." Or he may be made fun of in front of other people. Maybe other family members don't bother to listen to him. Sometimes they will laugh at his ideas, or simply fail to encourage and support him when he needs it. Quarreling is another way we may make the other person feel like a blob. When we can't win our argument easily, we will change our tactics and try to make the other person feel bad about himself, or less intelligent than us. When we are attempting to lower the other person's self-esteen, we are quarreling. This is our way of letting other family members know that we feel they can't live up to our oughts. If we are doing this in our home, we need to think about where we would be if God treated us this way—if he made us live up to His standards. We would never make it! The whole message of salvation is that God sent Jesus to die for us because we *can't* live up to His standards. When we, as God's children, fail to live up to His standards, He doesn't make us feel like blobs. He continues to accept us, to love us and to forgive us.

Another way families establish their relationships with each other is on the basis of *fear*. Specifically, this is usually the fear of rejection. This works in the following way: when a person does something to cross another family member, that person rejects the one who has crossed him. You've probably heard parents say to their children, "Go to your room." What they're saying is: "You're not good enough to be in my presence. Get away from me. I can only accept you if you live up to my expectations, my standards for you. So get out of my presence because you have not lived up." Nobody likes to feel rejected. So fear of rejection is what keeps many people in line and dependent on other people in their home.

The Silent Treatment

One common way of rejecting a spouse or a child is to give him or her the silent treatment for a day, for a week, for a month. After years of counseling, I'm still always amazed when a couple comes to me and they say, "We have not spoken for two months." Sometimes when I've listened as they've started to dump on each other, I've realized that silence was a lot safer. And yet, to exist in the presence of another person and try to punish them through silence is damaging to any relationship.

We also find marriages in which one person is trying through gifts or some good behavior to get back into the other's favor, but it isn't working. Here are two examples from the Scripture. In 2 Samuel, chapter thirteen, we read about a situation that occurred between David and his son, Absalom. Absalom had killed his half-brother, and so he fled and left the area for a while. Finally, one of David's men came and told him about it. David became convicted about the fact that one of his sons was still being treated as an exile, so he said to his man, "Behold, I grant this. Go and bring back the young man, Absalom." But because of the fact that Absalom had committed such an awful sin, he added, "Let Absalom go to his own house, and let him not see my face." Notice the rejection. Absalom went to his own house and did not see the king's face for two more years. David forgave Absalom in a limited way, but he continued to reject him. "You can come back into town, but I don't want to see you." The later outcome of this story is that Absalom led a rebellion against his father, as a result of which Absalom was killed. David's unresolved intense feelings are expressed in 2 Samuel 18:33: "And the king was deeply moved, and went up to the chamber over the gate and wept, and he said, 'Oh, my son, Absalom, my son, my son, would God I had died for you, my son!' " David finally accepted his son, but it was too late. Absalom had lived there for several years, not knowing that his father loved him because David did not accept him as he was. Thank God He accepts me "just as I am."

Gracious Acceptance of a Family Member

How do our family members know that we love them or that we forgive them if we are not willing to put our arms around them and verbalize our feelings to them. You might be thinking that the other person wouldn't like it or wouldn't respond, but you'll never know unless you try. A positive example is in the story I like to call, "The Forgiving Father." We usually call it, "The Prodigal Son," but I think it's misnamed. We read how the son went off, taking what belonged to him. He squandered it all and ended up living with the pigs and eating what they ate. One day he decided that he was going to get up and go home: "And he got up and came to his father, but while he was a long way off, his father saw him and was moved with pity and tenderness and he ran and embraced him and kissed him" (Luke 15:20). Sometimes as husbands or wives, as parents, we sit there and we wait for the other person to come to us. We don't make the first overture. We seem to be saying, "You have to convince me that you're sorry and that you want forgiveness and that you're going to be a changed person, and I've got to have a guarantee that you will never do that again." There are no guarantees, except the word of that person. In order to forgive a person or to love a person, we have to be willing to run the risk of trusting him or her and being hurt again. The risk is always there. But if you don't take it, what's your alternative? You really don't have one.

In Jesus' story the father brought the best robe, the honor robe, and he put it on the son. He brought out the fattened calf and said, "Let us have a feast and be happy and merry because this, my son, was dead, and he is alive again; he was lost and is found"

(Luke 15:24). Do we have the same attitude when a family member repents and admits his or her mistake? Is it a time of joy? Or do we still have a heavy heart and a lack of trust? It is true that if we reach out and trust, we may be hurt again. But our model in forgiving others and not continuing to blame them is what God has done for us. Difficult? Yes, especially when we try it ourselves. But it is not so difficult when we rely upon the Lord's power to work through us.

Joseph Cooke described the home that is dominated by God's grace:

> Here is a home where love and acceptance are not meted out on the basis of merit. Instead, the parents have somehow conveyed to the child's deepest awareness that their love is not dependent upon his being a good child. Their love is unconditional, unchanging, irrevocable. Somehow he knows that they care about him when he's up, when he's down, when he's good, when he's bad. It is not that they are content with his failures and wrongdoings. They care deeply, and they are not willing to settle for irresponsibility and hatefulness on his part. But their unconditional acceptance and love create in the child both the desire and the capacity to please them and to become the kind of person they long to have him be.[2]

FOOTNOTES

[1]Joseph Cooke, *Free for the Taking* (Old Tappan, NJ: Fleming H. Revell, 1975), page 29.
[2]Ibid., page 27.

3

MORE GRACE IN THE CHRISTIAN HOME

". . . this grace in which we stand . . ."

One important implication of grace is that God grants us status as co-heirs with Christ. I don't know if you've ever spent much time thinking about what it means to be a full heir with someone else. God is making us a member of His family forever because of His grace—not because of anything that we have done, but simply because of His grace.

In 1 Peter 2:9 we are called a chosen possession. That is how God looks at each one of us. We are a chosen possession for Him. We are also considered "children of the King." The titles that are given to the children of a king are "prince" and "princess." What would happen to a person who is struggling with his self-concept or self-image, so that he does not feel like he is worth very much, if he were to consider the fact that God sees him as a prince? We're co-heirs with Christ because of His grace. But unfortunately, many of us do not treat ourselves as co-heirs. We do not treat ourselves as princes or the princesses. We mistreat ourselves, we dump upon ourselves.

Treating Each Other as Co-Heirs

Look at this in the context of the family. Do we treat other family members as co-heirs? If you are in a marriage where you are believers, have you ever realized that there is an equality between you and your spouse because both of you are experiencing the grace of God? The same is true of your children; they are co-heirs with you. Do we treat our family members on the basis of this equality? We may even go one step beyond the immediate family: Have you ever considered that your in-laws are co-heirs if they know Jesus Christ? Do we see this equality, and do we respond in this way to one another? It's really an exciting thing to be able to say to a family member, "You know, we all stand in the same position before God because of His grace. That's why I can treat your needs as of equal importance to mine."

Enabling and Respecting One Another

In our homes, this aspect of grace is demonstrated by respect and enabling, rather than intra-family competition. Unfortunately, within some families competitiveness dominates. Occasionally, this is even fostered by parents between their own children. They pit one against the other. Or one spouse may want always to be in control, on top of the situation, rather than uplifting or building each other up. By contrast a truly Christian home is characterized by *respect* and *enabling*.

I wonder if you have ever taken the time to look into a dictionary for definitions of either of these words. I hadn't until recently. This is what I found. The word "enable" means "to make possible or easy."[1] So, if our home is dominated by a desire to "enable" one another, we will always try to assist them to achieve whatever it is that they are working toward. We will do our best to make it easy for them to be a part of our family, to grow and develop in Christian maturity, instead of being a blockage in their way.

The word "respect" means "to consider worthy of high regard."[2] In a Christian family we ought to look at another family member with the inner attitude that this person is worthy of high regard. That is sometimes difficult, especially if the other's behavior is somewhat obnoxious. Your children, your teenagers, your spouse—they're all imperfect, and sometimes they will behave in an obnoxious manner. But in those moments, perhaps we could consider the fact that this person is a born-again individual and therefore is a co-heir with Christ and a prince or princess in the sight of God. Then we are more likely to respond to him or her with respect.

One of the questions that each of us should answer is this: Am I blocking the road to development of my family members, or am I helping them to grow? In 1 Thessalonians 5:11 it states that we are to "encourage one another, and build up one another," to edify one another. And in Ephesians 4:12-16 we're told that we should help nourish one another.

The Role of a Servant

The basic principle is that a Christian home is characterized by respect and enabling, rather than by competition. But what does that mean in actual practice? Let me suggest several possibilities. One of the ways in which we can assist other family members and really demonstrate the fact that the grace of God is part of our life is to learn to assume what we call the role of a *servant*. This means that part of the process of growing as a Christian is to develop into less of a ruler and more of a servant.

In Philippians 2:3 we read: "Do nothing from factional motives—through contentiousness, strife, selfishness or for unworthy ends—or prompted by conceit and empty arrogance. Instead, in the true spirit of humility (lowliness of mind) let each regard the others as better than and superior to himself—thinking more highly of one another than you do of yourselves" (*Amplified Version*). This is one of the main passages that I use in training marriage and family counselors. In fact, in the margin of my Bible I have written next to this verse, "This is the counselor's attitude toward the counselee." It's very easy for a counselor, a psychologist or a psychiatrist to sit back with a judgmental or a superior attitude. Yet, if we were to put this passage into practice, we would see the person that God has brought into contact with our lives in the proper perspective. We would see ourselves as servants.

In verses 4 and 5 of this same passage it says, "Let each of you esteem and look upon and be concerned for not merely his own interests, but also each for the interests of others. Let this same attitude and purpose and humble mind be in you which was in Christ Jesus—Let Him be your example in humility" (*Amplified Version*). If we took this passage seriously, one of the ramifications would be that we would look to the other person with a desire to discover what his needs are. What are the needs of your child? What is the need of your spouse? The person who is trying to play the servant role will endeavor to meet those needs, rather than only showing concern with meeting his own needs.

Another passage which discusses the role of a servant is Ephesians 5. Many of us are familiar with this passage because it deals with the husband-wife relationship. Unfortunately, there has been some teaching which has distorted the meaning here with the result that the burden of responsibility has been put upon the woman. Actually there is more instruction here for husbands than for wives. A key verse is: "Husbands, love your wives, just as Christ also loved the church and gave Himself up for her" (Ephesians 5:25). This makes it clear that the husband's role is not that of a dictator or a dominater, but rather that of a servant. Jesus gave His life for us. He gave his life for the body, for the church. The husband is to love his wife as Christ loved the church, that is, in a sacrificial, self-giving way. The husband is to follow the model of a servant.

Nourishing and Cherishing

One of the arguments used in this passage is worth

special attention. Verse 29 says, "For no one ever hated his own flesh, but nourishes and cherishes [carefully protects] it." Nourishing the other person is part of our responsibility as a member of a family. "Nourish" means to give something or someone else the best possible care that you can. It does not mean to give just enough care to keep the object of your nourishing alive, so that it can limp along and exist. When you plant a rose in your garden, you don't give it just barely enough water, just enough nutrients to keep it alive. If you are any kind of gardener, what you want to do is to give it the utmost care. That's what "nourish" really means. Now, apply the same meaning of nourishing to how we relate to other family members. Are you giving them everything that is possible so they can really develop and blossom and grow to their fullest potential. This is what God wants for each one of us, and we are part of a family so that God can use us as activators, to help this process along in the lives of other family members.

Cultivating One Another's Uniqueness

If we respect and are trying to enable other family members, we will do all we can to help them develop their uniqueness and potential. The problem is that over the years within a marriage we tend rather to keep our partners from being their unique selves. Think back to when you were dating your future spouse. You discovered that he or she had some characteristics that were just their own—uniquely theirs. In fact, this uniqueness made them all the more attractive to us: "Isn't it wonderful that you have all these special qualities. It's tremendous!"

Some of this person's unique characteristics were used by us to complement some of the deficits in our own life.

Then we got married, and somehow a change occurred. What before we called "uniqueness" we began to see as "differences." Instead of enjoying their specialness, we tried to make them like us. "You know, I really never noticed this before we got married, but in some ways you are quite different from me. You think differently, you approach things differently, you do things differently. I'm right and you're wrong." After marriage we begin to equate differentness with wrongness. We cannot stand to have someone else act and think differently, because we are threatened by this. We are threatened because we feel that one of us may have to change, and maybe it's going to be me. So we begin to build the case that we're right and it's the other person that's wrong. We begin to pressure the other person in an attempt to change him and make him into a revised edition of ourselves. My concern here is that in doing this, could we be denying the uniqueness of our partner and thwarting the development of his or her spiritual giftedness?

But as we become more secure because of our relationship with Jesus Christ, we have greater freedom to allow the people around us to be different from us. We have a greater security, and this allows us to be less threatened by their "differentness." We begin to see how two, or three, or four different people within a family can magnify each other because of their varied characteristics.

Now, I'm not talking about behavior or attitudes which are different in that they are contrary to Scripture or to the healthy functioning of a home. Sometimes a person will complain, "I'm a neat person, and I like things in order. I'm not really compulsive about it, I just like some degree of order. But the person I'm married to lives in total disorder. He comes in, throws his coat on a chair, leaves one shoe in the hall, drops something else in the bedroom, leaves the newspaper laying around. And he just says. 'That's just the way I am—you'll have to learn to accept me. That's my uniqueness.' "

Let's run that kind of behavior through the grid of Scripture, and see if it can be seen as a legitimate way of acting. Included in the list of the fruits of the Spirit, in Galatians 5:21-22 is self-discipline or self-control. This means that if the Holy Spirit is in a person's life, there ought to be some degree of orderliness and self-discipline. Otherwise, we will create more work for other people, and that would not be helping them. Furthermore, a disorderly person is not developing to his own fullest potential.

I have found people who say they like disorderliness in their lives, but there is often a strange contradiction. When they begin talking about what they want for their children, it's not that at all. They want them to be neat, fastidious, right on the line, everything put in order, and they're frustrated because the children aren't developing in that direction. Actually, they are probably just following the model they see within the home.

"Making Allowances Because You Love One Another"

Let me share with you a key passage of Scripture which I believe really brings into focus this whole idea of uniqueness and acceptance of individual differences within our families: "Living as becomes you—with complete lowliness of mind (humility) and meekness (unselfishness, gentleness, mildness), with patience, bearing with one another and making allowances because you love one another" (Ephesians 4:2; *Amplified Version*). This last clause, "making allowances because you love one another," certainly applies to the matter of respecting individual differences. In other words, because of my love for you, I can accept that you will do things differently, that you will think differently. It's all right, I don't have to try to force you into a mold. In an unpublished article entitled "Conflict—Agony or Ecstasy?" the author made this statement:

> In the midst of the marital struggle, the honeymoon dream vanishes and the despair over the old relationship comes up for reexamination. Suddenly, each spouse turns his eyes away from the partner and looks inwardly and asks, "What am I doing to my partner? What is wrong with me? What am I misunderstanding? What must I do to rescue this marriage?" If honestly asked, the answers are not far behind. I really married my wife because of her difference. It is not my job to make her over, but rather to discover and to value that difference. But before I can do that, I must accept my difference and I really need her to help me discover my uniqueness. My task is not to mold her into a beautiful face, but to participate with her to discover that beautiful face even as we discover it in me. How arrogant of me to think that I could shape another human

being. How humble it makes me to realize that I need to yield to another and, thereby, be changed. Our relationship will change both of us in a process of being shaped into a form far more beautiful than either could imagine.[3]

Joseph Cooke expresses the same truth this way:

Some people seem to have an almost irresistable urge to reform or improve their partners in some respect. The wife wants to make her husband more socially acceptable, or to get him to take more responsibility around the house. The husband wants his wife to be a better housekeeper, or to be less of a gadabout. And so the attempt at reformation begins. Sometimes even the tiniest habits seem to require corrective action: the way one dresses, the way one walks, the way one squeezes a tube of toothpaste. I'm not, of course, suggesting that any of us have spouses that need no change. All of us need to change and grow in hundreds of different ways. The problem comes when the husband or wife appoints himself or herself a Committee of One to see that the necessary change is enacted, and in doing so says, in effect, "You must change; I can't really accept you as you are until you get busy and do it." The result is that grace is smothered and all genuine desire for love-motivated change is undercut.[4]

And James Fairfield writes:

We try to change people to conform to our ideas of how they should be. So does God. But, there the similarity ends. The way in which we are trying to get other people to conform is far different than the way in which God works with us. Our ideas of what the other person should do or how he should act may be an improvement or an imprisonment. We may be setting the other person free of behavior patterns that are restricting his development, or we may be simply chaining him up in another behavioral bondage. The changes God works in us are always freeing, freeing to become that which He has created us to be. As Paul described the process to the Christians at Corinth, "Now, the Lord is the spirit, and where the spirit of the Lord is, there is freedom, and we are being transformed into His likeness."[5]

It is not our job to take on the role of reformer in our relationship with our spouse. The Holy Spirit can do a much better job and we need to learn to trust Him. To show respect to people within our family, to be free to enable them, we must first develop a security within ourselves. Then we can begin to encourage other people to be themselves, to develop their uniqueness, to develop the potential which is within them.

Helping Our Children Become Individuals

Now, let's take this one step further and talk about

how it will apply to how we, as parents, relate to our children. Do we really enable our children and our teenagers? Do we seek to discover their unique potential, or do we try to force them into our own mold? Proverbs 22:6 is a fairly familiar verse, but let me share it with you from the *Amplified Version*, because I think it gives the clearest meaning of that passage. "Train up a child in the way he should go (and in keeping with his individual gift or bent), and when he is old he will not depart from it." Many times we have heard teaching about this passage to the effect that all you have to do is train a child in a certain way, and when he's old, he will not depart from it. That means that if we give him a lot of Christian instruction, we have a safeguard—even if he wanders away, eventually he will come back. That is *not* the correct meaning of that verse. Chuck Swindoll has written a book entitled *Knowing Your Child*, in which he gives a thorough exposition of this passage.[6] He shows that it teaches parents to try to find what is the individual bent or leaning of the child and encourage that child in that direction. We should help him channel and use his individuality rather than pushing our mold upon him.

For example, here is a boy who really is much more musically and artistically inclined than athletically inclined. But, as happens quite often, his father is very sports-minded and keeps trying to force his son in that direction, rather than encouraging him toward his individual bent.

One child in your family may be fast-reacting and does things very rapidly. Then a second child comes along, and he may be very slow and methodical—perhaps a little more thorough. You may try to get the fast one to slow down and the slow one to speed up, but maybe that isn't the best. This is often a problem in small town schools. There may be numerous children within a family and every two years or so one of them comes into a given teacher's class. She remembers the previous brothers and sisters, and unconsciously expects the new child to follow the same pattern. One child in your family may be a genius. His schoolwork comes easy. But for another child schoolwork may be a real chore. Yet, he might have giftedness that the first one didn't have. The wise parent will try to discover the unique gifts of each child and then help him use it.

Assuming you want to relate to your children in an enabling way, what are some of the things you can do to help prepare them for the difficult world they will face? Let me make a couple of suggestions to you. One proven method of instilling values and morality into children is what can be called the innoculation approach. Now, the innoculation approach follows the medical model. Most of us have had a smallpox vaccination, and this means that we were given a very minute dosage of smallpox so that we become immune to it. Then if we ever hit the disease head on, we're not going to be overwhelmed by it. The innoculation approach to teaching values and morality is based on the belief that by the time a child gets to the age of nine, ten, or eleven, his overall approach to life will already have been developed and instilled in him by the verbal teachings and the modeling of his parents. At that stage of his life, the parents need to sit down with the child and talk to him about the various other value systems he will encounter as he goes out into the world.

They can easily use a sort of case-study approach, asking the child, "What do you think *you* would do if you were ever faced with that? How do you think you would handle it?" or, "What would you do if a kid said such-and-such?" By doing this they are exposing the child to a small dosage of different moral systems, so that when he hits them head on, he will not be overwhelmed or taken by surprise. He will have already thought about them and can anticipate what is going to be said to him and what his response can be.

Approaching the Teen Years Creatively

If you have teenaged young people, have you ever sat down and talked with them about how they are going to handle the situation when they are out on a date and the person they are with begins to come on too strong sexually? Have you ever talked with them about what they will say, what they will do? Quite often parents tell their children to have a strong standard of morality, but they don't show them how to hold onto that value system when they find themselves in difficult life situations involving a lot of peer pressure. This applies to boys as well as girls because a lot of fellows in our day are getting pressure from some of the girls that they are dating. Things have changed in the past fifteen years.

When young people get to the age of fifteen or sixteen, there are some important changes the parents need to relate to. When our daughter hit the age of sixteen, there were two very important events that took place: she was allowed to date, and she could obtain her own driver's license. Both of these new developments have the potential to create neurotic, anxious, up-tight parents. So I started to anticipate how I would respond about a year-and-a-half in advance. I wanted to help her be as prepared as possible. I wanted my wife and I to help enable her. We're not going to be out there with her on a date, we're not going to be out there when she's driving, so what can we do to really help her develop standards and hang onto them?

I was particularly conscious of this need because of my experience: (1) I was a youth pastor for seven years and worked with about 300 teenagers and their parents as they went through these crises; and (2) I had been working in the area of family therapy, where I saw a lot of things that disturbed me. From these perspectives I saw how many parents wait until their young person is already involved in a number of these activities, and then they decide they don't like what they see, and they try to pull the young person back and establish rules and guidelines. This leads to a real power struggle and the family has a hassle on its hands.

In an attempt to avoid these problems, Sheryl began working in advance toward these two important events in her life. I want to share with you one of the things we have worked out together to guide us through these changes. I am not saying that this suggestion is the ultimate answer. It is not perfect, for we are not perfect parents, nor do we have a perfect home. We go through some of the very same struggles that you go through, so this idea might stimulate some thinking in your mind regarding your teenagers. I'm sharing this with our daughter's permission, because I don't want to do anything that would embarrass her.

Negotiating an Agreement

In our family we worked together on developing a driving agreement, so that when Sheryl began driving on her own, the guidelines would be clear—she would know how much latitude she would have, she would know what the restrictions were. And we as parents would also know the ground rules that she had accepted. We each put our suggested guidelines down in writing, then came together and did some negotiating. In the end we came up with what we call a "driving agreement" and a "dating agreement." The important point to remember is that we did not go in and say, "O.K., here is what you are going to follow." We did not impose it upon her. We all had an opportunity to put in our ideas and then make some changes. Since then, every six months or so we take a look at the agreements and make changes as they seem necessary. Changes are especially likely in the dating agreement, for the situation varies as Sheryl becomes older.

If you consider making an agreement with your teenager, don't make the mistake of taking a model developed in another family and imposing it on yours. You have unique people in your family, which means that what works for another family is not going to work for yours. This means that you have to do some creative thinking and be willing to hear suggestions that you may not want to hear. And the agreement that is finally negotiated may be a whole lot different from what you yourself may have wanted. You may tend to be a little adamant when you see some of your pet ideas rejected.

When we finally settled on our agreement, we each

signed it as an indication that everyone knew what it said and agreed to it. This really helps out, because if one of us says we never talked about a certain issue, we can go back and say, "Look, we did talk about it; I guess you've forgotten it. Let's review it."

A Driving Agreement

Here's the driving agreement we came up with. The first item was: "Before using either car, I'll ask my mom or dad if I can use the car and explain the purpose for using it." The reasoning behind that was that many young people are just driving without any purpose. Secondly, the agreement said: "If I want to go somewhere for myself, my homework and practicing has to be completed." That part of it our daughter put in. Joyce and I wanted to add the word "thoroughly."

The third item was: "During my first six months of driving with my own driver's license, the radio will not be used while driving." There was no negotiation on that; it was a dogmatic pronouncement from Dad. My reasoning was that when kids are just starting out driving, their skills have not yet been refined, and I believe they need to pay full attention to what they are doing. I had some mixed feelings being so dogmatic about this, but I've gotten feedback from both insurance people and police officers and they agree with it and think it's valid, so I feel a little more comfortable about it.

Continuing in the driving agreement, we wrote, "During school I'll be allowed to drive to church on Wednesday nights, but I can't take anyone home without prior permission. I will not allow anyone else to drive the car under any circumstances. I will be allowed up to thirty-five miles a week, and after that, I must pay for any additional mileage." When she wrote her version of that item she put in thirteen miles a week. She didn't know how to judge distances, so we upped that, because she would have been paying quite a bit in no time at all. "I will not carry more than five passengers at any time in the Plymouth or more than three in the Audi.

"Upon receiving my driver's permit, I will be allowed to drive to church and local areas when either Mom or Dad is along." Our daughter put that one in. I added the next one. "I will assist in driving for extended periods of time on our long vacations under all types of driving conditions." I wanted her to have an opportunity to drive on good roads, bad roads, in rain, on gravel roads, and I wanted this to happen when we were there so that she could talk it over with us. I wanted her to make mistakes in our presence, rather than later on. Her test came when we were driving back from our vacation the first year she had her license. She drove 250 miles the last day on a two-lane road, having to pass cars and trucks.

The driving agreement also said, "I will not give rides to hitchhikers under any conditions, nor will I accept any ride if I should have difficulty with the car. I will either wash the car myself or have it done every three weeks. I will pay half of the increase in insurance cost, and in the case of an accident, I will assume half of the deductible cost." She earned the insurance money the first summer by helping me paint the house.

A Dating Agreement

Our dating agreement included this item: "I agree

to memorize and be able to explain the meaning and the application of the following verses before beginning to date." And we listed 24 or 25 passages.[7] The rationale for this particular part of the agreement came from her dad, simply because I believe in the power of the Word of God to stabilize and guide our life. This grows out of my own experience as a teenager at Hollywood Presbyterian Church. We used the Navigators' "B" rations and "IR" rations. One particular verse stabilized and helped me through my high school years: "There hath no temptation taken you but such as is common to man, but God is faithful . . ." (1 Corinthians 10:13). I can remember time after time when the Holy Spirit activated that verse, and it came to mind just when I was at the point of having to make a decision for right or wrong. To be very honest, there were times when I didn't like that verse coming to mind, but it was there, and it was a beautiful guide and control for my life. I have seen many other ways in which the Scripture has affected my life, and I really believe that we ought to be encouraging our children and our young people to build their lives and their stability on the Word of God. That's why this item was included in our dating agreement. I wanted to be sure my daughter had the resources that would enable her to express her fullest potential.

FOOTNOTES

[1]*Webster's Seventh New Collegiate Dictionary* (Springfield, MO: G. & C. Merriam Co., 1966), page 272.

[2]Ibid., page 732.

[3]Abraham Schmidt, "Conflict—Agony or Ecstasy?" (unpublished article).

[4]Joseph Cooke, *Free for the Taking* (Old Tappan, NJ: Fleming H. Revell, 1975), page 127.

[5]James Fairfield, *When You Don't Agree* (Scottdale, PA: Herald Press, 1977), page 195.

[6]Charles Swindoll, *You and Your Child* (Nashville: Nelson, 1977), pages 27-36.

[7]The passages we listed were as follows: John 16:24; 1 Corinthians 10:13; 1 John 1:9; Proverbs 3:5-6; 1 John 5:14-15; Matthew 7:7-8; Ephesians 4:29; 1 Thessalonians 4:3; Philippians 4:8; 1 John 5:4-5; 1 John 4:4; Ephesians 6:10-11; 1 Corinthians 15:57; Romans 8:28; 1 John 4:10; 1 Peter 1:15-16; Ephesians 5:4 (Amplified translation); Jeremiah 33:3; Isaiah 40:29-31; Isaiah 41:10; Isaiah 43:2.

4

TRIBULATION IN THE CHRISTIAN HOME

". . . we also exult in our tribulations . . ."

**A Home Full
of Christians**

**EXULT IN
TRIBULATION**

We welcome stress as a teacher of patience.

Greater patience proves we have handled stress successfully.

Proven character makes exulting in hope responsive.

A Christian Home

**SUPPORT IN
TRIBULATION**

Mutual support in stress develops interdependence.

Interdependence develops greater personal responsibility.

Proven responsibility builds self-respect and intrafamily respect.

Because we are justified by faith we exult in tribulation. The dictionary defines tribulation as "great pressure" or "distress." But God makes it possible for the justified person to "exult in tribulation." Exultation is extreme joy. The Greek word means literally "to leap up"—that's the kind of joy the Word of God says you can have because of your relationship with Jesus Christ, even when you are going through difficulties.

Trouble Comes to Everyone

If I were to ask you the question, "Do you really know what pressures and stress are? Have you experienced some kind of tribulation?" Almost everyone would be able to answer yes. Facing troubles and trials is an inevitable part of life. Many people try to avoid life's pressures, but sooner or later they have to be faced.

In the Old Testament, for example, we have the example of Moses. He was trying to lead the people, but they constantly "grumbled and deplored their hardships" (Numbers 11:10-15). In other words, they were always griping and complaining. "Moses heard the people weeping throughout their families, every man at the door of his tent," so he said to the Lord, "Why have you dealt ill with your servant?" In other words, "Why me? Why have I not found favor in your sight that you lay the burden of all the people on me?" He was blaming God for the personal trial he was experiencing. He felt free to tell God how he really felt: "Have I conceived all this people—have I brought them forth that You should say to me, 'Carry them in your bosom as a nursing father carries the sucking child' to the land which You swore to their fathers to give them? Where should I get meat to give to all these people? . . . I am not able to carry all these people alone, because the burden is too heavy for me. And if this is the way You deal with me, kill me, I pray You, at once and be granting me a favor" (*Amplified Version*). He came right out and shared his concern and his uptightness with the Lord.

Actually, God had not really given him all of that responsibility to carry. Moses was trying to take on too much. Once before he had been trying to do it all himself. He was attempting to counsel all the people himself, so his father-in-law—and here is a positive example of a good in-law relationship—said, "Moses, what are you doing here trying to carry all of this by yourself; you're going to wear yourself out. Let's bring in some other people to help you." And that's the way that problem was solved.

God responds in much the same way here, saying, "Choose seventy other people to help you at this time." There are cases where we are responsible for the stress that we experience in our lives, because we do not allow other people to assist us. In such situations stress can be reduced if we simply stop trying to do everything alone.

Stress Teaches Patience

But at other times God allows stress in our lives specifically to teach us patience. Some of us seem to need more stress than others in order to learn patience. But we can be assured that there is always a purpose for stress, whether it is coming directly from God or is indirectly allowed by Him. And knowing that stress can be purposeful is a cause for us to be joyful and welcome it, or as the Scripture says, "to exult in tribulation."

Because we are justified, you and I can come to the place—and notice the words I am using here—we can *come to the place* where we welcome stress as a teacher of patience. I find that many people are bothered because they don't instantly feel this joy. "What is wrong with me? Am I not spiritual enough?" Our Christian life is a growing process; most things don't happen instantly. But if we allow God to work in our lives we will begin to see the gradual change. This week I've got a little more patience than I had last week. There is a steady growth in patience. As we begin to see this we can welcome stress as a teacher of patience.

Some people feel strong enough to handle their own problems by themselves, and they expect others to do the same. So they fail to reach out and help other family members during times of stress. But in a truly Christian home, there is a system of mutual support that develops interdependence. In other words, we learn to rely upon one another. I have the knowledge that if I'm upset or hurting or going through something difficult, I don't have to carry the burden alone. I may, like Moses, have a burden that is too heavy for me, but I am carrying it alone because I have failed to share it with the other family members. I have put them into the position of being mind-readers. Instead, I need to learn to say, "Hey, my day was really upsetting, and this is the burden that I'm carrying. I want to share it with you so that you will be aware, and then we will be able to pray about it together." This is how we can grow in support for one another in times of tribulation.

When you begin to see greater patience in your life,

this will prove to you that you are learning to handle stress successfully. You are witnessing the emergence of a character trait. If you find that you are much more patient now than you used to be, you can feel reassured that the Lord really is doing His deep work in your life. Maybe you haven't arrived at where you'd like to be, but you're growing.

Bearing Burdens in the Family

In a Christian home, this kind of interdependence develops greater personal responsibility and helps each individual mature. If I feel I am accountable only for the tribulation that I am going through personally, and I don't care about the tribulation that Joyce and Sheryl and Matthew are going through, I am being very selfish and I am showing that I have not assumed some of the characteristics of responsible adulthood. But if I am truly concerned about them and what is bothering them, I will grow in responsibility through being concerned for others. I will become more faithful in praying for them. I might come up and ask one of them, "How are you doing? Are things working out?"

Our daughter might be facing an algebra exam. I might not feel that is really "tribulation" or great distress, but she probably does. It's weighing upon her mind. So, how can I, as a father, help her with that? I know that in the case of algebra I can help her best by not actually doing her homework with her, because I'd foul her up more than she is already. Algebra is not really math to me, it's Greek! But there must be some way I can help bear her burden.

Tribulation Can Be the Doorway to Joy

Quite often we face our worst kinds of tribulation at the very time when we feel least able to handle it. Last year, for example, I had an experience of tribulation that soon proved to be a blessing in disguise. Not all stress or tribulation is going to turn out all right so quickly. We might be carrying it for a long time. Maybe we will never see the positive results in this life. But on this occasion, I submitted a paper to be presented at the state convention of marriage and family counselors in San Francisco, and it was accepted. I was scheduled to speak at 1:00 P.M., so I got on the plane at Long Beach Airport at 7:00 A.M. It normally takes about an hour to fly up there, but weather conditions were bad, and we couldn't see a thing. So, we flew around for an hour, then for another hour. Finally, the pilot said, "We're running out of gas, so we're going to have to land in Stockton." After a two hour wait, we refueled, got back into the air and again headed for San Francisco. It was 1:30 P.M. before we landed, and I missed the chance to give my presentation.

Now, ten years ago, if that had happened, I wouldn't have needed an airplane; I'd be flying high without it at that point! I would have been unbelievably uptight and tense. But instead, I found myself thinking calmly, "You know, there's the possibility that I won't get there. O.K., if I don't, I don't." I was reassured by this, because I realized how I had grown in the past ten years. It was an evidence to me that God was working in my life.

I never got to the convention. I went in and changed my tickets, and got a place on a flight right back.

When I walked over to the plane, a lady came up to me, and I recognized her as someone whom I had met two weeks before. She said, "I'm here to bring someone to the airport who is going to Long Beach for a speaking engagement." I said, "Who is that?" The lady informed me that it was Ann Kiemel, the author of several popular books. She was to speak at my church the very next day. As a result of my "tribulation" I was able to enjoy about an hour and a half with this fine woman. I had read her books and heard her tapes, but I'd never had the opportunity to meet her. We had a delightful time sharing Christian fellowship at leisure.

Choosing Between Possible Attitudes

You might be facing some stress this very day. If not, you certainly will in the future. You will have to choose between several different types of possible responses toward tribulation. We cannot always choose our circumstances, but we can choose the attitudes we will have toward those circumstances.

Here are some common attitudes that people have when they are experiencing pressure. One popular response is to decide that life is hard and cruel, and to become angry at God for allowing such a thing to occur. That might be your initial reaction to difficult situations, and then you might feel guilty over having such an attitude. Well, maybe we just need to accept that instant response and then begin working from there. This is similar to the very normal angry responses people have to the discovery that they are terminally ill. Anger is just one of the natural stages such a person will go through in what we call their "grief work." They predictably go through various phases of anger and depression, but eventually they are usually able to turn the corner to a better attitude.

There is a man in the Old Testament that God used a great deal—David. He experienced deep feelings, and he poured them out to God. As we read the psalms, we find that he reacted to tribulation in a variety of ways. Sometimes he was angry; sometimes he was down; other times we see how he was able to praise God in the midst of difficulties.

Some people respond to difficulties by closing themselves to life and allowing their difficult circumstances to make them bitter and resentful. Their bitterness is expressed especially toward others who seem to be enjoying life. "Look at those guys down the street who are living irresponsible lives. They don't go to church, and yet, they've got everything together. Here I am, I've been trying to be faithful, trying to love and serve the Lord, and look what happens." This is a very common response.

We will do better if we remember that anger comes about because we're either frustrated, hurt, or afraid. If we can learn to bypass some of our anger and get back to its cause, we will be better able to deal with our difficulties.

Another common response is to turn anger and hurt inward. We may blame ourselves for the mishap and spend the rest of our years punishing ourselves for it. That's how depression develops. Depression can be a side-effect of anger turned inward.

Or, we might respond to difficulties by deciding that life has no meaning and doubting God's existence. We may wander in unbelief, turning our backs completely on God and saying, "You're not there; otherwise, you would have done such-and-such." We project our own theology onto God and tell Him who He ought to be and what characteristics He should have. I would encourage you to read either *Knowing God*, by Packer,[1] or *The Knowledge of the Holy*, by Tozer,[2] to remind yourself of the attributes of God as they are revealed in the Bible. Otherwise, you may fall into the trap of trying to remake God in your image.

The Best Response to Tribulation

There is one other possible response to difficulties or tribulations. We can move ahead in faith and experience the life-giving resources that God has for us. Let me share with you another experience from the life of David in the Old Testament. In 1 Samuel, chapter 22, we read about how David responded to persecution: "So David departed from there and escaped to the cave of Adullam." In other words, he ran for his life because Saul was after him and intended to kill him. "And when his brothers and all his father's household heard it, they went down there to him." Verse 2 is a beautiful description of the type of people who had gathered around David: "And everyone who was in distress or in debt or discontented gathered to him." There were about 400 distressed people gathered around David. Some of us might identify with them. There were people who were in debt. Some were discontented. And here was David. People were trying to kill him, and he looked around at this crew of loser individuals. They were probably very downcast, very upset, grumbling and griping.

What could he say to a group like that? David's words to them are recorded in Psalm 34. Imagine yourself as one of these 400 depressed individuals sitting there waiting to hear what David is going to say. Some of them probably fell off their rocks when they heard this: "I will bless the Lord at all times; His praise shall continually be in my mouth." A strange statement, we might think. But by this time David had worked some things through in his mind, and he was at the point where he could honestly say, "I will bless the Lord at all times; I will praise Him." Verse 4 of the psalm is interesting: "I sought for the Lord and He heard me and He delivered me from all of my fears." In essence, what David says is, "I just opened my life to God and prayed to Him and poured out my feelings. God answered and my fears were relieved." David doesn't say that God took him out of the circumstances, that God got him away from all his enemies, that He got Saul off of his case. No, he was still in the midst of the problems, but God delivered him from his fear.

I can imagine that some of the people who heard him were really wondering what was going on. How can anyone with David's kinds of problems be so positive? Years before David might not have been able to handle this as he did now. He had grown. Learning to respond to difficulties in a constructive way is a process. You and I have the opportunity to grow through this process in our lives, but we should not just grow by ourselves. What about the other family members who are sharing our lives? Are they aware of what we are going through? Do we reach out and get them involved in our growth through trials?

Some Tribulation May Never Go Away

There is an excellent book that explains how even extreme tribulation can become the means of exciting growth. It is *Run from the Pale Pony*, by William Pruitt. In a very fascinating way this author uses an analogy to share what has happened in his life. In the foreward of the book he writes:

> About thirty years ago, one of my joys as a boy was to ride a white horse named Prince. That proud, spirited stallion carried me where I wanted to go, wherever I bid him to and at the pace which I chose. I don't have to explain to horsemen the feeling of strength, even authority, which comes from controlling such a powerful animal. Nor need I expand upon the excitement I felt when I galloped him at full speed, or about the quiet pride that came when I twisted him through the corkscrew turns of a rodeo exercise. After all, he was mine and I trained him. Those experiences are part of my heritage. My cherished white horse was gone and seldom remembered about fifteen years later. It was then that I encountered a completely different kind of a horse. When I first became aware of the specter, its shape was too dim to discern. I know only that I had never seen anything like it before. Too, I know that I had not sought any such creature, yet something different was with me wherever I went and that shadow would not go away. I told myself, "Really, now, you're much too busy to bother with something that seems determined to disturb you, get rid of it." And I tried to will it away. No matter what I did though, the specter followed my every move. Furthermore, the

harder I tried to lose it, the clearer the creature's form became to me. My uneasiness changed to anxiety when I realized that this unwanted shadow had a will of its own. The chill of fear came when I understood that it had no intention to leave me alone. Without further warning, it began to communicate with me openly one day, and in a harsh voice which was almost rigid with animosity, it spat out, "You can no longer go where you want to go when you choose at the speed you pick. That's true because I will give you weakness instead of strength. Excitement and pride? Never again will you have them like before. I plan only confinement and disability for you. And I will be your constant companion. My name is Chronic Illness." At the time I heard it speak, I shrank back from actually seeing it face to face. It spoke harshly of miseries which were inverse to joys with my white horse named Health and the bitter irony was reflected in the form of a malicious creature. Chronic illness took the shape of a stunted misshapen pony. Its shaggy coat was pale in color, streaked with ages old accumulation of dark despair. But, unquestionably, the most frightening feature of the animal was its overwhelming glare—its glare-eyed stare which held me helpless. The pony's wild eyes started restlessly from side to side, yet strangely were unblinding. This book is written first of all for those people who have met the pale pony face to face.[3]

There are many possible forms in which the "pale pony" might come to us, including serious physical or mental illness, accident, war injuries, etc. Whatever shape the pony takes, the results can be quite similar. This particular person's pale pony was multiple sclerosis. He sensed that the disease was increasingly affecting his life, but his story is the story of hope. He realized that he had a number of years before he would be completely disabled, and realizing that he wouldn't be able to carry on the type of work he had been in, he went back to college in a wheelchair. He earned a Ph.D. in economics and began to teach on the college level.

This is not a book about giving up, but rather about fighting back and winning. It's a very honest book, telling of the pain and the hurt and the turmoil, but its emphasis is on faith and hope. I shared this book with a friend of mine who read the section I quoted to a lady in a wheelchair. He discovered that she too had multiple sclerosis and had been going through much difficulty and depression. As a result of reading the book, her attitude changed dramatically within a week. She came back to him and said, "I have ordered three copies, because I have other friends who are in the same state that I am."

Consider It All Joy

You see, the key issue is our response. We could honestly say, "God, this isn't what I wanted in my life, I didn't plan for this." But it's here. How are we going to respond to it?

Let me again share with you the verse that has meant so much to me in my life, for it helps me put into perspective what I can do when difficulty comes. This is one of the verses which I ask couples in premarital counseling to build their marriage upon. "Consider it all joy, my brethren, when you encounter various trials; knowing that the testing or the trying of your faith produces endurance" (James 1:2-3). Now, it's one thing to read a passage like this out of the Word of God and say, "Well, that's fine," but it's another thing to put it into practice. What does the word "consider" or "count" actually mean? What kinds of trials is the Bible talking about here? Does this refer to sins that we may get involved in and for which we are responsible?

The word translated "consider" or "count" means "an internal attitude of the heart or the mind that causes the trial and the circumstance of life to affect us adversely or beneficially." To put it very simply, it means, how you look at a problem. You can look at it and say: "That's terrible. That's totally upsetting. That is the last thing that I wanted for my life. Why did it have to happen now, just a week before vacation? Why me?" The other way of "considering" the same difficulty is looking at it and saying: "It's not what I wanted or expected, but it's here. There are going to be some difficult times, but how can I make the best of them." Don't ever deny the pain or the hurt that you might have to go through. But always ask, "What can I learn from it, and how can it be used for God's glory?"

It Takes Work and Discipline

The verb tense that is used here indicates a decisiveness of action. It's certainly not resignation:

"Well, I'll just give up. I'm just stuck with this problem. That's the way life is." If we resign ourselves, we will sit back and not put forth any effort. No, the verb tense actually indicates that you will have to go against your natural inclination to see the problem in this particular way. There will be some moments when you won't see it like that at all, and then you'll have to remind yourself: "No, I think there is a better way of responding to this. Lord, I really want you to help me see it from a different perspective." And then your mind will shift to a more constructive response. This often takes a lot of work on your part.

The Word of God makes it clear that our thought life can be controlled. We have the promise of the ministry of the Holy Spirit in helping us change thought patterns, but on the other hand, the Scripture says we are also responsible for making the decision to change. Peter says, "Gird (strengthen) your minds" (1 Peter 1:13). The Greek word he uses indicates mental exertion, and this means that we should forcibly put out of our mind anything that is going to hinder our Christian walk. Another way our passage in James 1:2 might be translated is: "Make up your mind to regard adversity as something to welcome or to be glad about." We have the power to decide what our attitude will be.

When Circumstances Are Beyond Our Control

An understanding of the word "trial" is very important in this passage. A trial is a kind of trouble or stress that comes from outside of us. James is talking about the kind of stresses or disappointments or sorrows or hardships that are not the result of our own sin or foolishness. We did not have anything to do with the fact that this difficulty has come upon us. We have not purposely put ourselves into a dangerous situation. Now, we might have contributed to it, but the situation itself was not the result of our action. You might be driving along, obeying the laws, when somebody comes through the signal and smashes into the side of your Corvette. You could have avoided the problem by leaving your car in the garage, but you did not really do anything to deserve the accident.

Sometimes parents get kind of discouraged because they feel that they're doing everything they can for their children, trying to follow what the Word of God has to say, trying to be consistent and loving, and all of a sudden, the children do exactly what they've taught them not to do. Maybe we as parents have failed to take into account our children's free will. They've got minds of their own, and they are likely to make some choices with which we don't agree.

The Family Is the Acid Test

James says that when we respond to trials in a positive way, the result is an increase in patience, or endurance. When we are under pressure, he encourages us not to try to escape, but to stand firm. You're right there in the midst of it, and you're remaining firm and you're growing in patience. That's the Christian response to trials.

Reading this passage out of the Word of God and living it are two different things. If we decide to put it into practice, it may be that God is going to allow us to experience more and more stressful situations so that our patience can be really exercised and developed. And quite often God puts us through our major trials within our homes. The real test is whether or not we live in patience with one another in our family. Quite often, we can be very, very patient out there with the people we work with or the people in our church. We may be able to share with them how we have been able to deal with this problem. And then we go home and all of a sudden, we aren't exhibiting that same kind of patience. We snap at family members and are very irritable. Maybe that is the true test of whether we are growing in patience. "Hey, I have been able to work through trials so that my patience is effective even in my family."

I have been basically an impatient person most of my life—with others, with my work, with myself. I like to get things done yesterday. I have difficulty sometimes in taking on too many projects and then being frustrated because they're not all done right away. One of the ways God has been developing patience in my life and in that of my wife Joyce is through having our son Matthew in our home. Matthew is a brain-damaged, mentally retarded child. His retardation is very severe, and he is about a year-and-a-half old mentally. The doctors say he will never advance beyond a mental age of two-and-a-half years. Having Matthew in our home has meant a number of adjustments, a number of stressful situations. It has also been one of the most effective avenues by which God has taught us to exult in tribulation within our home.

It has helped us to learn to depend upon one another and not be so independent. One of my obvious characteristics when I was first married was my independence. I know this grated on other family members, and sometimes it still does, because it's not all gone and may never be. Nor should I necessarily try to get rid of it entirely, because there is a healthy place for independence. However, when it overrides other people's needs, it begins to hurt. Because Matthew has been in our home, I have learned how much I need others.

Many different things have contributed to our growth in patience. Praying for a child to walk for three and a half years, and then being there, with the whole family, the night he gets up and walks. Not hearing any real words for seven or eight years, and then, all of a sudden, listening to hear him say "baby" or "good," even though you still don't know what meaning it has to him. But in a sense, even our questions about his meaning are part of the process of learning. There is an element of hope and encouragement because now that we have heard a word that you and I understand, we can begin the slow process of learning to communicate with him. Matthew has brought to us numerous experiences of growth in patience.

Responding to Tribulation as a Family Unit

In the last two years, however, we began to realize that Matthew's presence in the home was beginning to affect us in other ways. As he was getting older and heavier, his care became more demanding, to the place where we were experiencing more and more stress in the family. My wife had the heaviest burden. Some nights he would go to sleep well, but other nights he wouldn't. The basic issue we have had to face is whether it is best for Matthew to be with us for the rest of his life, or to be in a home where he would get even better care and have more contact with other children. Which would be better for him? And what would be best for our family life?

I had assumed that I was further down the road in thinking this way than my wife was, but when we finally got to talking about it, I realized that she had thought it through more thoroughly than I had. I went through some anxiety and confusion because I was further back than Joyce was. So, for the past two years, we have talked and prayed about it.

About a year and a half ago, we visited a home for children like Matthew which we really liked. We put Matthew's name on the waiting list, and then we went home and prayed that the Lord would open this door. A while later a counselor from the school district came over and said, "It's down to about a six to twelve months wait." Patience! And then finally a call came from the home, and they said that a bed would become vacant the first of November. They asked us to bring Matthew in for an interview. All of a sudden, here it was. We were face to face with the real loss of Matthew from our home. Joyce and I went through all kinds of new struggles. Were we ready at this time, especially with Matthew just getting over mono-nucleosis and bronchitis? So we went to the interview with all kinds of mixed feelings. For an hour, we were interviewed by four of the people there, and it was really a good experience. Our fears were relieved and we had peace about the decision.

After the interview they said, "Well, we'll talk it over; there is a little concern about whether he'd respond in school. We'll call you." Now we had to have patience again. That first day I think I asked Joyce two or three times, "Have they called?" And then the second day, you know how your mind works: "Well, since they didn't call in the first day or so, maybe they're trying to figure out how to say no." It's interesting how we can take that beautiful gift from God called imagination, and we can use it to create rather than solve problems.

And then the third day the phone rang. I beat Joyce to the phone. The person on the line said, "This is so-and-so from Salem Home," and my stomach just tied up in a knot. But the response was, "We would like to take Matthew on a trial basis and we hope that it will work out permanently." Talk about answers to prayer! For us that was a real time of rejoicing.

God's Guarantee—Growth Through Trials

The last two years of working through our feelings about this have been stressful, but it has been a growing process. When you have made a decision like that, there is always a little hidden thought: "Could I have done more? Could I have done it better? Is this best? Am I neglecting my motherly or fatherly duty?" But then we can go back in our minds and see how God has brought us to this point through deep struggles. We can be secure in what He has already taught us through tribulation.

I would just like you to take a moment to look at your life and identify the hurt or the disappointment or the stress or the hardships that you might be experiencing. Ask yourself, "How can this be used for my growth? How can this be used to develop greater patience? How can God be glorified through this?" I would ask you to commit this difficulty or feeling to God, and thank Him in advance for what He can do and will do in your life through tribulation.

FOOTNOTES

[1]J. I. Packer, *Knowing God* (Downers Grove, IL: InterVarsity Press, 1975).

[2]A. W. Tozer, *The Knowledge of the Holy* (New York: Harper and Row, 1975).

[3]Ronald Pruet, *Run from the Pale Pony* (Grand Rapids, MI: Baker, 1976), pages 9-10.

5

HOPE IN THE CHRISTIAN HOME

". . . and we exult in hope . . ."

A Home Full of Christians

EXULT IN HOPE

We stand on God's promises of eternal life with Him.

We anticipate God working in and through our lives.

Our self-images are being transformed into God's glory.

A Christian Home

IS A HOPEFUL HOME

It is characterized by trust in one another's promises.

Family members are served rather than used.

We can remove our masks confidently.

A further result of justification is that you and I can exult in hope. As we discussed in the last chapter, the Greek word translated "exult" means literally "leaping for joy." I don't know if you've ever had that experience where you just had to leap because you were so joyful. I remember when Bruce Jenner won the decathlon in the Olympics. As he won the final event, he jumped straight up in the air for joy. This is often seen in sporting events when a football player or a baseball player makes a tremendous play—he'll just jump up and down.

Leaping for Joy

I suppose that there is something that is so significant for each one of us that it would cause us to leap for joy. For me it is fishing. A few years back when we were going through the Grand Tetons on our vacation, I was working a deep pool in Cottonwood Creek. I knew that there were lunker trout in the pool, because I could see their huge shapes shimmering below the surface. They would come up and look at the bait, and then swim away. But after a long while, one of them came rushing out, grabbed the bait and nearly took the pole and me with it. We fought for a long time and finally, when I got him out, I saw that he was a big nineteen-inch Yellowstone cutthroat trout. My hands were shaking as I held him. I let out a whoop that people heard in the cabins half a mile away. Some of them came running down to the creek, thinking I had fallen in or something like that. But I was so excited I hadn't stopped to think about people's reactions.

That's the kind of joy our Scripture says is a possibility for all of us because of what God has done for us in Jesus Christ. We can literally leap for joy. And our leaping for joy is based upon God's faithfulness in keeping His promises.

Trusting and Being Trustworthy

One of God's great promises is that we are going to be with Him and will be made like Him. We can read about this in 1 Corinthians 15:50-58. Doesn't that make you want to jump for joy?

Because of our relationship with God in Christ, we have confidence in Him and we can trust Him. That is the basis for our future hope. We can be sure that He will not let us down. His promises are trustworthy. And surprisingly, the reverse is true also. God continues to open up and trust *in us*, even when we are unfaithful and we let Him down. As you and I become more and more like the person of Jesus Christ, we become more trustworthy individuals. In other words, people can trust us more, they can have more faith in us.

This is a very important basis of Christian fellowship. We are better able to maintain faith in God's people, even when they have let us down because we have a mutual trust relationship with God. Have you ever been disappointed in a fellow believer? Maybe you have trusted him, and all of a sudden your trust has been violated. Does that mean that we are never to trust him again? No, we have the opportunity to forgive him, and then reach out and trust him again.

In a Christian home, this principle is in operation when we trust one another's promises. If your child tells you, "Mom, I'll be home tonight at 6:30," do you take that at face value, or do you add a little comment, such as, "You'd better be," or "If you're not, you know what's going to happen." The added phrase shows lack of trust. Instead we may say, "Thank you for letting me know. I really appreciate that because it eases my mind." That indicates family trust.

What happens when one of the family members violates our trust? Are we willing to open our lives to be hurt again? They've let us down, and that proves that they're not perfect. But we're not perfect either. So because of our trust in God, we rely upon their word again. We can give them the benefit of the doubt and see them as innocent until proven guilty. Sometimes we seem to have the opposite approach to our children. We see them as guilty, and their innocence has to be proven.

Expecting God to Work

A second aspect of exulting in hope is the anticipation that God is going to work in and through our lives. Now, none of us is as much like Jesus as we should be or as we're going to be. So we can anticipate that God will be working continually in our lives. He's going to refine some of those rough edges, which really need to be smoothed out.

We make allowances for God's unfinished work in our own life, but do we take the same approach for family members? "God is going to work in the life of my husband. He's going to be working in the lives of my children. He's going to be working in the life of my parents, my in-laws, my brother, my sister." That's part of being a Christian home. It's believing in God's purpose for one another.

Hope is a very important word. Let me give you some definitions: "hope" means "trust" or "reliance"; it's "desire accompanied by expectation"; it's the "happy anticipation of good." Hope does not refer to present reality, but to the expectation that God will finish what He's started. Hope should govern our own Christian life. Hope should dominate the way we see potential in the lives of others.

When couples come to me for pre-marital counseling, I ask them, "What are your expectations for your marriage?" Occasionally someone will say, "Oh, I don't have any. I'm just going to let it evolve and develop as it does. My spouse can do whatever he'd like to." When I hear that, I keep asking and probing, because I know this person really has some expectations. Otherwise, he wouldn't get married. He's hoping that certain needs are going to be fulfilled.

To help couples clarify this, I have each of them write down twenty-five expectations that they have for their marriage. Then I ask them to take each expectation and write a paragraph on how it would affect them if that expectation were *not* fulfilled in their marriage. Finally, I have the couple share those expectations with one another. This does a great deal to eliminate future conflict.

You probably have expectations of other family members. Do they know what they are? Have you ever shared them? Have you ever asked your husband or wife or your child, "What expectations do you have of me as a family member? If you tell me, I might be better able to meet them, if it's at all possible." If you don't share your expectations, you're using a device that is called "emotional insulation." "If I don't ever hope again, I won't get hurt." But, unfortunately, if you don't hope, you will not only miss out on pain; you will also miss out on happiness and delights of life. There is a purpose in the conflict and in the pain that we go through, and expectation and anticipation is very, very important to our enjoyment of the end product.

Cooperating with God in Meeting Needs

Because we anticipate God's work in our lives and the lives of our family members, we can place ourselves at the service of our family members and become more of a servant to the family than a user of the family. We can allow ourselves to be the agent of their growth, because God is giving us the assurance that our own growth will come in the process.

If we have decided to serve our family for our mutual growth, we need to begin to discover the needs of our family members so that we can try to meet them. In a book entitled *No-Fault Marriage*, the author points out: "The amount of satisfaction you get from your marriage is determined, in large part, by how well you and your partner agree to meet certain of each other's needs. It also depends on the degree of opportunity and encouragement you get from each other to meet some of your own needs."[1]

How do you discover the needs of your family members? Begin by recognizing that we all have certain kinds of needs in common. Abraham Maslow developed a model of basic psychological needs we have.[2] He said that people have five general kinds of needs: physiological needs, safety needs, love and belongingness needs, esteem needs, and self-actualization needs. Maslow put these in the form of a pyramid, because the lower level needs have to be met first. For instance, physiological needs (air, water, food) must be met before we can begin to meet the higher levels. If you don't have those things, you can't even live.

Now, let's liken this to a family relationship. We'll focus on the husband's role. Most husbands endeavor to help their family members meet their physiological needs. I don't see too many husbands who are not providing sufficient food, air or water for their families. I think they're pretty good at that. Most husbands are also quite effective in helping family members meet their safety needs. They make sure that the brakes are good on the car, the tires are up, locks are on the door, the rug is tacked down so that people don't trip on it.

But What About Their Deeper Needs?

However, where we as husbands have a tendency to fail is in meeting the top three for other family members. They have love and belongingness needs. How can we show them that we love them? That they belong? That they're really accepted? Have you ever asked family members, "What is it that I can do to give you a sense of being loved, of belonging?"

Too often spouses take the attitude that they will show love toward their husband or wife in their own way, and that should be acceptable to the other person. Judson Swihart pointed out the need to discover how our partners want to be shown love:

> The golden rule now takes on a more subtle but more important meaning. It is not just what you do unto others as you would have others do unto you. Matthew 7:12 is not saying that you behave toward your spouse only as you want him or her to behave toward you. It is saying in essence seek to understand and meet the unique needs of others just as you want your unique needs understood and met.[3]

This becomes very practical in our everyday relationships:

> If your wife feels loved when you help with the dishes, then roll up your sleeves and reach for Joy (the detergent as well as the feeling). If your husband feels loved when you meet his emotional needs, then find out what those are and begin to help fulfill them. Your spouse will never get the message if your expression toward him or her is the language that's meaningful only to you.[4]

There are many small things we can do without much effort. For example, many times I have seen a couple enter a meeting, and the husband leaves his wife standing at the door, while he goes over and starts talking with his friends. He may fail to introduce her to a group in which he is better known than she. That can make her feel left out. She doesn't belong.

There are two ways we can communicate love—verbally and nonverbally. My friend Rex Johnson (author of chapters 6 and 7) travels a lot. When he unpacks, he often finds all sorts of little notes his wife has planted in his luggage and throughout his clothing. They may be love notes, or cartoons, or secret messages. Sometimes it's sort of embarrassing when he opens up the suitcase. There pinned to an undershirt or underpants is a little love note or something, and he slams it shut! One day we were on an airplane together, and when he was going through his coat pocket he found a note he'd overlooked. It was a series of symbols that translated into "I love you so." I could tell that he had a very warm response to that simple little message. These creative expressions of love add a little bit of delight to their relationship.

Emotional Vitamin Pills

We all need to become a little more creative about sharing love. I learned this little trick from one of my students at Talbot Seminary. I went down to the drug store and I bought 52 of the little cellulose capsules that usually contain medicine. They can be bought empty. During some vacation time, I wrote out a little note for each one of those capsules on pieces of variously colored paper. I conned Sheryl into helping me stuff them, because it was a laborious job. Then for Joyce's birthday I gave her a bottle full of all these little pills. On the label it said they were one-a-week (not one-a-day) vitamins. Every Sunday she got to pull out one pill and open it. One time it might say, "I love you," or "Kiss," "Dinner at McDonald's" (That was one of the better ones!) or "I'll spend a half-hour just doing what you want to do this week," or "We'll go to a nice restaurant." The amazing thing is that the weeks when I felt that I was the most pressured and didn't feel I could spend much time at home, invariably Joyce would draw one of the little capsules that had a more time-consuming promise in it. But that was good, because it helped me put things in priority.

If you would like a book that will give you some good, creative ideas about the romantic area of the marriage relationship, there is a new Bible commentary on the Song of Solomon, entitled *Solomon on Sex.*[5] It's a delightful book, with good scriptural teaching and helpful practical applications.

The Need to Feel Self-Esteem

An even higher level of need is the need for self-esteem. We need to be able to feel good about ourselves, to like ourselves, to see ourselves as persons of worth and of value. What does it take for the people around you or your family members to believe that they are persons of worth? What is it that you can do to help them feel good about themselves? It might be that we can make some encouraging comments to them that will help them see potential in themselves that they have overlooked. Or we may contribute to their self-esteem simply by not taking them for granted.

Author Charles Shedd has made it a practice over the past twenty years to give his wife one positive compliment every day. Every week he has endeavored to give her one brand new compliment that he has never given her before. You can't imagine the number of men who have asked me, "Has he listed them in a book so I can buy it?" No, he hasn't put his compliments in a book. That would rob you of your own creativity.

I have known a number of couples who have had good success with what they call "a caring day." On a particular day each week they try to do as many as possible of the positive things they know their spouses would like them to perform. The theory behind this is that if you increase your positive behavior toward family members, the negative things you might otherwise be doing don't stand a chance. There is so much satisfaction in relating to someone in a positive way that negative behavior will soon be squeezed out.

One couple came up with the following lists to help

each other express caring in practical ways. Here is the wife's list:

> Greet me with a kiss and a hug in the morning before we get out of bed; bring me pussywillows; ask me what record I'd like to hear and put it on; reach over and touch me when we're riding in the car; make breakfast and serve it to me; tell me you love me; put your things away when you come in; if you're going to stop at the store, ask me first if there is anything I want or need; before we go to sleep, rub some part of my body with full concentration; look at me intently when I'm telling you something.

And here's the husband's list:

> Wash my back; smile and tell me you're glad to see me when you wake up; fix me orange juice; call me at work; acknowledge my affectionate advances; invite me to expose the details of my work; massage my shoulders and back; touch me while I drive; hold me when you see that I'm down; tell me that you care; tell me about your experiences at work every day; tell me that I'm nice to be around.

That's just a sample. In your family, you would need to work out your own ideas of how love can best be shown to you and your self-esteem built up.

Becoming All You Can Be

The highest level of need is self-actualization.

That basically means "meeting your potential." Putting that into Christian terms, this might mean discovering the spiritual gift that God has given each of us. In a family this can be very important. Maybe it's a wife seeing that her husband has a strong desire for further schooling and expressing her willingness to go back to work so that he can return to school. Or maybe it's the husband saying to his wife, "You quit college in your third year, and I know that you've got a desire to finish. I would be willing to babysit three nights a week if you would like to go back and complete your schooling."

I feel that in the years that Joyce and I have been married she has not really had the opportunity to develop her gifts in art. I hope that some of the changes now occurring in our family structure will give her the opportunity. That is, if she desires to do it. I have no right to force or push her. I can only give her the opportunity to develop that area of her life for her own enrichment. It's important for us to try to help our family members discover their potential, their area of giftedness, so that they can be more and more satisfied in themselves, and, even more important, so that they can serve the Lord more thoroughly.

What We Have to Look Forward to

Self-actualization has a lot to do with the development of our self-image. I think we could say that another reason for exulting in hope is that our self-image is being transformed into God's glory. Do you know what that means? In 2 Corinthians 3:18 Paul talks about how we gradually take on the character or the ways of God. Our transformation into God's image is a continual process in this life, and when our life ends, it will still not be completed. As we live together in a family, we should realize that there is a process going on. Our self-images, hopefully, are being built and built through every life experience.

In the context of 2 Corinthians 3:18, Paul is talking about Moses. He tells us that after Moses had been with God, his face was shining; there was a radiance about it. He was beaming and glowing. But after a while, the shine began to fade. So what did Moses do? To keep the people from seeing that the glory of his face was fading away, he put a veil or a mask over his face. To some degree or another, most of us wear a mask. And the purpose of wearing a mask, especially within the context of the church, is so people will not notice that we are not as much like Jesus as we'd like to be. Unlike Moses, we are not trying to cover up a fading glory. Ours is a permanent glory, because it has been given to us by the Holy Spirit. This means that within the church, as well as within our families, we can begin to take off our masks and reveal who we really are.

In my practice in counseling I often hear a wife or a husband say: "I have been married to this person fifteen years, and yet I feel like I'm living with a stranger. I don't know what's going on inside of him, or what makes him tick." But if God really is present in our lives, why can't we be free to open up and say, "Look, here is where I don't feel all put together. Here is where I don't feel very secure."

Being Honest About Present Shortcomings

Let me give you an example of how this created a

little conflict in our marriage for a while. When it comes to plumbing, I am worse than an amateur. We had a faucet that was incessantly dripping and Joyce periodically suggested that I fix it once and for all. I thought I should be able to do it; I had the tools and it was really an easy job. But I was procrastinating, and it was getting worse and worse. Finally Joyce's suggestions became a little too strong to ignore. The two of us stood in the bathroom and watched as a steady stream of water ran from the faucet. I finally said, "Look, the reason that I'm not tackling that is that I just don't feel I know what to do when it comes to plumbing. I'm afraid of botching it up even worse." She stood there and she said, "Well, thank you for telling me that. I never knew you felt that way. If I'd known that I wouldn't have been after you so much. Now I've got a better understanding of what's going on inside of you." The problem was quickly solved. I called the plumber and we had it fixed right away. Previously she had been seeing my behavior as resistance against her suggestion and procrastinating. Now she was was seeing that my behavior was coming from my sense of inadequacy. She wasn't a mind-reader, so she couldn't know that until I took off my mask.

Helping Each Other Feel Like Somebody

Maurice Wagner, in his excellent book, *The Sensation of Being Somebody*, talks about what goes into making up our self-image.[6] There are three aspects of our self-image: belongingness, worthiness and competence. Belongingness means having a sense of security and identity with others who love, accept, and support us. Worthiness means being affirmed as a person of value, cherished and respected. Competence means gaining a sense of achievement and being affirmed as an able person. It's important within a family that we get feedback from one another to help us in these three areas. But even beyond that, the main reason that you and I can have a sound self-image is that God sees each one of us as a new person in Christ. Lloyd Ahlem summarizes what God has done for us:

> The writers of the Scriptures are careful to point out that when God looks at you and Jesus Christ, He sees you as a brother to His own Son. Because of the work of Christ, all the ugliness of humanity is set aside. You are worth all of God's attention. If you were the only person in the whole world, it would be worth God's effort to make Himself known to you and to love you. He gives you freely the status and adequacy of an heir to the universe. This is Agape love, the unmerited, unconditional favor of God for man. We achieve our adequacy through this unceasing love. We do not become sufficient, approved, or adequate; rather we are declared to be such.[7]

I hope all of us who are men heard the last statement, that God declared us to be adequate or competent. Many men try to build their feelings of worth and self-esteem upon how well they do in their vocation. That's why they often allow it to take priority over their family. But, you know, there are days when I don't really do a good job, and I know it. Even at such times I am a person of worth and value, and I can feel that I belong because of what God has done for me. I can assure myself that there will be other days in which I will do better work because of what I have learned through this one day.

FOOTNOTES

[1]Marcia Lasswell and Norman M. Lobsenz, *No-Fault Marriage* (Garden City, NY: Doubleday, 1976), page 26.

[2]Abraham Maslow, "A Theory of Human Motivation" (*Psychological Review* vol. 50, 1943), pages 370-376.

[3]Judson Swihart, *How Do I Say I Love You?* (Downers Grove, IL: InterVarsity Press, 1977) page 75.

[4]Ibid., page 76.

[5]Jody Dillow, *Solomon on Sex* (Nashville: Nelson, 1977).

[6]Maurice Wagner, *The Sensation of Being Somebody* (Grand Rapids, MI: Zondervan, 1975), page 32.

[7]Lloyd Ahlem, *Do I Have to Be Me?* (Glendale, CA: Regal, 1973), page 71.

6

LOVE IN THE CHRISTIAN HOME

". . . the love of God has been poured out within our hearts . . ."

A Home Full of Christians

GOD'S LOVE POURED IN

God's evaluation of us becomes perceptible.

God's perfect love replaces fear.

Worship is a blessing to us as well as to God.

A Christian Home

GOD'S LOVE EXPRESSED

Affection for each other is expressed rather than assumed.

Family circle of love replaces role expectations based on fear.

Time together as a family is precious rather than perfunctory.

One of the tremendous benefits of the fact that we have been justified by faith is that the love of God has been poured out into our hearts.

God loves you. Is that startling? Oh, you've heard it before. But what does it mean? The knowledge that God loves you is just the beginning. God actually wants you to sense His love in your heart, in your life. He wants you to feel it in your bones. It's one thing to know that God loves you. It's another thing to feel loved.

How Do You Know When Someone Loves You?

It's one thing for a son to know that his father loves him. When I was a child, I never doubted that my daddy loved me. But you know, there were special times when I really *felt* that my dad loved me. When he grabbed a mitt and I grabbed mine and we'd pitch and catch the baseball, I felt that he loved me then. I knew that he loved me all the time, but then I *felt* that he loved me. It was one thing to know that my mom loved me. But sometimes she cooked MY meal. I mean she cooked a meal just for me, not for my dad, or my sister. She made my favorite things—not just on my birthday, either—and I felt loved, special.

God wants you to know that He loves you. That's why He writes so much about it in Scripture. From the Bible you can be assured that God loves you. But there is another dimension of God's love that can only be appreciated from experience. God pours His love out in our hearts so that we can feel it.

This love of God poured into our hearts has important implications for the family. As I begin to feel God's love, I can express that same love to others. Furthermore, the fact that God's love is poured into our lives makes His evaluation of us perceptible. We begin to understand how important we are to Him. And as a result, we can lift the self-image of other family members whose view of themselves is unrealistically low. Do you realize that you are worth the precious blood of Jesus Christ? That's what Jesus paid for your redemption, and other members of your family are worth the same high price.

Why We Feel Unlovable

James Dobson comes to the conclusion that about 90 percent of us have problems with our self-images.[1] We don't see ourselves as worthy. We see ourselves as inferior to the people we relate to. We receive this impression about ourselves from early experiences when we were tiny and powerless in comparison to our parents. The sense of inferiority usually settles in one or two areas: "I'm just too short," or "I'm too clumsy," or "I'm too ignorant." Once we have this basic impression of ourselves, we go through life finding people who will agree with us. When they do, they reinforce our feelings and the impression settles into our self-image. We go around saying "I really am ugly, aren't I?" And we find someone who will say, "Yes, you're ugly." I may go around saying, "I really am getting bald, aren't I?" And everyone says, "Well, your hair *is* thinning out." That confirms my impression of myself.

Now, when our impression of ourselves is accurate, that's O.K. But most of us don't give ourselves the benefit of the doubt. We begin saying things about ourselves that really are not true, and then we become those things. As a result, our self-image becomes lower and lower. This is what happens when we base our self-image on others' reaffirmation of what we think about ourselves.

How God Makes Us Feel Lovable

The strange truth is that God does *not* reinforce our image of ourselves. Rather, He tries to get us to agree with His impression of us. He refuses to reaffirm our faulty impression. He says: "Look, here's the way you are, and I want you to understand this view of yourself and to base your self-image on that. Here's what I want you to know about yourself. First of all, I made you."

Psalm 139 tells us that God knew us before we were conceived and that He knows us inside out. The word that is used in the psalm was the Hebrew way of referring to the deepest part of a person. The word actually means kidneys in the original language. God says, "I know all about your kidneys." Now why would God say that He knows all about our kidneys? Well, our kidneys are not among the parts of our body that we go around bragging about, are they? We might brag about our hair. We may fix it up and make it really look nice. We may do something to improve our face, such as grow a moustache or beard. And we wear fancy clothes to make other parts of our body more attractive. But we don't dress up our kidneys. There's not much we can do about them. They're a part of the body that we just sort of take for granted. But God says, "I know you so well that I'm even an expert on your kidneys. I know about your feelings of being too short or too bald or too thin. I know all about that. I made you. And I love you."

Secondly, God says, "I died for you. I loved you so much that I spilled my precious blood on a cross for you."

Thirdly, He says, "You're forgiven. Whatever has been in the past, you're now forgiven. You can have a self-image that's based on forgiveness." The idea of "I'm O.K., You're O.K." that is quite popular today would be much better expressed and lived by Christians in the words "I'm forgiven, You're forgiven." Do you realize how free we can become in our self-image when we begin to accept the fact that God really did forgive us? Because God forgave us, we can forgive each other. When we begin to sense who we really are as forgiven people, we can be freed up to forgive others.

God wants us to really *feel* that. It's one thing for Him to give us a high evaluation of ourselves by saying, "You're forgiven, you're worth the precious blood of My Son Jesus Christ." It's another thing to feel that forgiveness deep within us. That's why God keeps pouring His love into our hearts. We tend to shut it out because our old self-image makes us feel we don't deserve it. We tend to truncate it. We tend to not want God to love us too much, or not want to feel God's love too much, because that might make us change a bit. But God wants us to change our self-image, so He keeps pouring love in.

Passing God's Love on to Others

That's the model we have to follow in our families. If we do to others what God is doing to us we will be constantly expressing our affection to the other members of our family. We won't be satisfied with the way we currently express our love. We will want to grow in love and in loving behavior. That's called "feeding" your love relationship.

One of the assignments that I like to give couples when they come for counseling help is to find a new way, one they've never used before, to express their love to their spouse, every day for the next week. People agonize over that. Sometimes I'll be teaching in Sunday School or at a camp on married life. One session may be on love, and another on sex. You'd think the topic of sex would be the threatening one, but it isn't. They can handle that. This is something that we have learned to do in the past few years. But when I turn to the subject of love, about some new things that you can try to develop creativity in the expression of love, people become very threatened!

Find New Ways to Express Love

Let me share some suggestions about expressing love that I've received from friends and counselees. One person tried the exercise of finding a new way each day to show his love. The first day he thought and thought before he came up with any idea. Then he went home that night and watered the plants. In all his years of marriage he had never done that, because they were her plants. But he could see that she was tired, so without a word he went out there and watered the plants. She noticed, but she didn't say anything. She thought that was really neat, but since he didn't say anything, she didn't either.

The next day he came and shared that with me. I said, "Great!" He said, "I don't know what to do next." I said, "I'll give you one suggestion, since you already came up with one of your own. How about buying her something that she has mentioned she would like?" He thought about it a minute and then said, "Yeah. Two weeks ago we were over at the shopping mall and she saw a blouse she wanted. Let's go over there and get it." So during our lunch hour, we went to buy the blouse. When he was discussing the size with the saleslady, she asked, "Is it for her birthday?" "No." "Well, then, is it your anniversary?" "No. I'm just buying this because I love her." The saleslady couldn't get over it. You could see that inside she was thinking, "I wish my husband would do that."

Well, he bought it—it only cost about $6.00 —wrapped it, and left it on her pillow with a little note: "Love, Rod." He had made plans to go to the ballgame with his son that evening, and his wife wasn't home when he left. When she came home, she couldn't imagine what the gift meant. "He's never done this before. It isn't my birthday. It isn't Christmas. It's not the 4th of July. What is going on?"

The next night he took home some construction paper. His wife was out that evening for a meeting. So while she was gone, he put together an "I-love-you card." It wasn't something that he bought from the store. This was his idea and he wanted to make it from scratch. On the front he pasted pictures of some of the things that she liked to do, making a kind of collage. On the inside he pasted pictures of some of the things they like to do together, including vacation pictures because they had just been talking about their summer plans. At the bottom he signed it, "Love, Rod."

Now she began to figure out that something was going on with this guy. Three nights in a row. The next night she found a one pound box of See's candy on her pillow, and she just had to get to the bottom of it. The following morning she sat down in front of him and said: "What's going on?" And he said, "What do you mean, 'What's going on'?" She said, "I can't figure it out. This has been the happiest week of my marriage. What are you doing to me?" He said, "I'm just learning to express my love." She responded, "You've always loved me," and he said, "Yeah, but I'm learning to *express* my love. I've gotten some help down at work and I'm just learning to express it." She said, "Keep it up!"

You know what happened next? He sent a dozen long-stemmed roses to her at work. There she was at her desk when a florist delivered the beautiful flowers. The card said, "Love, R." *She* knew who's initial that was, but the people she worked with didn't. They went out of their minds. "Who's R? It couldn't be your husband. Your husband would never do anything like that." The same day at *his* work he received a Western Union telegram. She had sent it prior to receiving the roses. The card said "You are the sunshine of my life. I love you." Now he was out of his mind.

These two have been married for seven years and all of a sudden in one week they began to express their love creatively. They have enjoyed their new relationship so much that he has made this commitment: "I am going to keep this up. I will find at least one new way of expressing my love every week for the rest of our marriage." I'd like to recommend that to you.

Making a Good Marriage Better

The expression of love must be creative. You must keep working at new ways of saying and showing "I love you." You've heard the expression "redeeming the time." Redeeming (buying back) the time simply means that when the going is good, that's the best time to work on your marriage. It's fine to say "I love you" in the middle of a crisis in order to reassure your spouse that you love him or her. But in the long run it's more constructive to say it when there is no crisis, no reason, no birthday, no Christmas. Is your marriage in a period of smooth sailing? Then this is the time to express your love in some new way, to bring new life to your marriage, to practice the art of loving. One of the things that gives an occasional boost to our marriage is for me to get up quietly on a Saturday morning and fix breakfast in bed for my wife. That isn't a big thing, because I'm not really much of a cook. I'll fix something I can handle, like oatmeal pancakes. That's one of our favorites. I'm very quiet so that she'll sleep through. Then the first thing she sees in the morning is me coming in with this tray full of food. Every time I do this it just thrills her! That's my way of saying again, "I love you, Honey."

She comes up with some creative ideas of her own. I travel a lot with the International Center for Learning. I'll do this about sixteen weekends between September and May. It means that I am gone from Thursday afternoon to Saturday evening. On Friday morning I'm only half awake because of the jet lag problem, but I have to get up and get at it. I start to put on my underwear, and I feel something strange. There's a little note inside. It says "I miss you." Later I'll pull out a towel and another little note falls to the floor. Another may turn up in my shirt pocket. I'll be half way through the seminar and I'll feel a piece of paper. I'll pull out a note that says, "I'm thinking about you today and I love you very much, Evie." Such little touches help to build the kind of expression in love that is always fresh and alive. Creativity may come naturally to you, so why not try it? Don't ever make the mistake of taking your love for granted.

Love Drives Out Fear

I John 4:18 says, "There is no fear in love; but perfect love casts out fear, because fear involves punishment, and the one who fears is not perfected in love." Perfect love casts out fear. It is very natural for us to fear God, and the fear of the Lord is the beginning of wisdom. But that is not the kind of fear we usually think of. The fear of the Lord that is the beginning of wisdom is the respect with which we enter into the presence of the Lord of the universe, sensing how great He is and standing in awe of Him. That kind of fear is the beginning of wisdom, but the kind that drives us away from God is not healthy fear. God doesn't want us to be afraid of Him, and that's why he pours His love into our lives and lets us feel it; His perfect love casts out fear.

Love Breathes Life into Marriage Roles

When we start living by that model in our family, a family circle of love replaces the role expectations that most of us live by. These role expectations are based on fear. Most of us have a series of roles by which we are bound. Maybe your major role is that of provider and father. Do you realize that you were a man long before you were a father? You were a person long before you were a father or a mother. You were a woman long before you were a bride or a wife. You were a man long before you were a husband. Those functions have hardened into our roles. A role is something an actor or actress plays. The person plays a role temporarily, but he continues to be the same person before and after. Unfortunately, many people fall into the pattern of living by roles. They confuse the role with the person. They are comfortable only when they are in their familiar roles.

The role of father is seen by most people in the following way: He is a person who has a wife and some children, goes to work to make the money for the home and has the last word in matters of discipline. The mother's role is to take care of all the rest of the household details. Part of the father's role might also be to read the newspaper while he's eating and watch television afterwards. The details of our role expectations vary, but most of us live up to whatever picture we have in our mind of what a father or a mother should be. Rather than carefully planning how we will fulfill our role, we have an idea what a father or mother should be like, and when we become one we step into that role picture. We may have gotten it from our own father or mother. In fact, most of us, no matter how much we rebel against our parents when we are teenagers, end up being parents pretty much the way they were.

You have probably heard about the woman who was preparing to cook the ham as she always had, when her daughter who was watching her asked, "Mommy, why do you cut off both ends of the ham before you put it in the oven." Mother said, "I don't know, but that's the way I learned to do it from my mother." So they went and asked Grandmother, "Why do you cut off the ends of the ham before you put it in the oven." And Grandmother said, "I don't know; that's the way my mother taught me." They went on to Great Grandmother and asked her the same question. Her answer was, "Well, because in our day we didn't have a pan big enough for the ham to fit in." We learn our role expectations from our parents, and we follow them without questioning them.

As Christians we should be aware of the fact that our role expectations are not only based on observing our parents, but also on the influence of culture. As a result, we tend to interpret the scriptural teaching on marriage on the basis of the roles that we've already settled upon in our minds. Romans 12:2 says, in the Phillips translation, "Don't let the world squeeze you into its mold." Or to paraphrase this even further, "Avoid stepping into the world's roles."

We have an alternative to offer. The world adopts male chauvinism as the proper role for men. We need to show the world that Christianity presents an alternative to male sex roles that subdue and put down women. By the same token, the world understands various female roles: the traditional submissive wife role, the newer women's lib role, the role portrayed in *Playboy* magazine. We need to show that Christianity offers an alternative.

I believe the Biblical alternative to the world's role expectations is the *circle of love*. Our traditional role expectations are built upon the Greek military model. In this model there is a straight line of authority. Each person is responsible to someone above him, who is his superior, and decisions are passed down in a straight line.

Love Frees Us to Submit to One Another

The world around Jesus well understood the Greek military system of roles. But Jesus came along and said, "That's not the way it should be with you believers. I've got a better way." In Ephesians 5:17 we read: "So then do not be foolish, but understand what the will of the Lord is." The will of the Lord is almost always in contrast to the world system. It is an alternative. So we need to become aware of and understand what the will of the Lord is. We should be prepared to hear something about marriage roles in the next few verses that is different from the world's system, an alternative.

And in verse 21 we find it: "Be subject to one another in the fear of Christ." Notice that this relationship of subjection is *two-way*. That's the difference between God's will for our marriages and the mold the world would like to squeeze us into. There is a submission role for both men and women. Many are all for the submission role of the woman. They can handle that. But this passage tells us that there is a submissive role for men that is just as important. We may try to filter it out so we can keep our worldly role expectations, but we can't find one type of submission here without accepting the other.

The kinds of submission that are assigned to husband and wife are very explicit. Wives are told, "Be subject to your own husbands as to the Lord." Some have tried to translate this, "Be subject to your husband as they are subject to the Lord." In other words, if they are not subject to the Lord, then you don't need to be subject to them. That's a mistranslation. The only sound interpretation is: "Be as submissive to your husband as you are to the Lord."

Now, the subject here is not the area of decision-making. He's talking about living your life in a style that pleases God. He's not telling us who should get the last word in an argument. He's describing an attitude of life. Wives should place themselves in a relationship with their husbands that is similar to the church's relationship with Christ. "Wives, be subject to your own husband as you are subject, the same way you are subject to Christ, for the husband is the head of the wife as Christ also is the head of the church, He Himself being the Savior of the body."

Let me illustrate what I mean when I say that this passage is not talking about who gets the last word. Let's say that I stub my toe. Now, if my head has the last word, my head should be able to say to my toe, "Don't hurt." My head doesn't have the last word. The toe keeps on hurting, and there is nothing my head can do that will alleviate the pain until my toe is ready to quit hurting. Sometimes men try to do that as head of their home: they try to say, "Quit hurting." But we do not have the last word on that. This passage is not talking about who gets the last word in decision making. But as the church is subject to Christ, willingly casting her lot with Him, that's the way wives are to be subject to their husbands.

Love Allows Us to Lead by Serving

Husbands, you have a role of submission too. But it isn't expressed in the same way. The passage doesn't say, "Husbands be submissive to your wives." It says: "Husbands, *love* your wives, just as Christ also loved the church and gave Himself up for her. Now, that gets us away from the role expectation kind of love, because it emphasizes a certain quality of love, rather than just quantity. The quality of love that reflects the spirit of Christ is servant love. The whole mission of Jesus was to be a servant. We read about this in Philippians 2:5: "Let this mind be in you, which was also in Christ Jesus: Who, being in the form of God, thought it not robbery to be equal with God: But made himself of no reputation, and took upon him the form of a servant . . . and became obedient unto death, even the death of the cross" (*King James Version*). Wherever Jesus' love is described in the New Testament it is servant love.

This passage tells men they are to love their wives in the same way, and that requires submissiveness just as a wife's role does. Men are to show servant love to their wives. That's not a very popular idea in America today, but we can't let our culture ("the world") define our roles.

I grew up in South America, where my folks were missionaries. We were not in a class above the people we were working with, but in that society we were expected to and we did have servant girls. It's a European-based concept, and is foreign to our American practice. We had servant girls before I was born, and I became aware of them when I was about five. I realized that, even though I was a five year old and the servant girls were young adults, they had to do what I said unless it was in conflict with what my parents had already said. If I asked one to make my bed, she had to make it. That's the way the society was constructed. She was our servant. Her job was to fulfill all of our wishes, to work for us, and what any of us said she was to do. That's submission.

A Circle of Love, Not a Chain of Command

If we men have come to the conclusion that God in His word has given us some sort of authority guide that makes us the last word in all family decisions, then we need to face again what this passage says about how we love our wives. When we do, we will see that our homes would be better described as a circle of love than as a chain of command. I have a problem with the image of a home where the husband is a hammer, the wife is the chisel, and the children are diamonds. You're supposed to be hitting your wife over the head, and that makes changes come about in the lives of the children. That's not the circle-of-love family that I see described in the New Testament.

The contrast between a chain-of-command home and a circle-of-love home may be diagrammed:

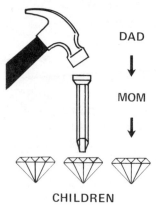

CHAIN-OF-COMMAND

DAD
↓
MOM
↓
CHILDREN

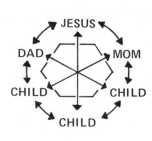

CIRCLE-OF-LOVE

JESUS
DAD   MOM
CHILD   CHILD
CHILD

BASED ON ROLES	**BASED ON CALLING**
EMPHASIS ON COMMAND	**EMPHASIS ON LOVE**
CONCERN FOR AUTHORITY	**CONCERN FOR SUBMISSION**
MOTIVE OF OBEDIENCE	**MOTIVE OF SERVANTHOOD**

All of us must reexamine the atmosphere in our homes. Is our relationship with one another based on *roles that we are fulfilling*, or is our relationship with each other based on *love that we are expressing*?

When Love Rules in a Marriage

God's love poured into our hearts also makes worship possible. Some of us keep trying to get a blessing out of worship. We come on Sunday mornings to receive a blessing. But that's not really the important thing about worship believe it or not. Worship is not primarily getting but giving. The important thing about our Sunday morning worship is that God is blessed. If we receive a blessing in the process, that's a bonus. And one of the wonderful results of the fact that God's love is poured into our hearts is that He blesses us when we worship Him. So if your worship tends to get dry, allow God's love to be poured out more fully in your heart. Then spend some time in the process of blessing God: "Bless the Lord, O my soul and all that is within me. Bless His holy name" (Psalm 103:1). You will find that you yourself will receive a great blessing in the process.

The principle holds true in family life as well. As long as you are concerned with getting, your relationship will be dry and unsatisfying. But when you seek to give other family members a blessing, you yourself will receive the blessing by-product. God's love poured out into our hearts and expressed in our families makes time together precious rather than perfunctory.

Most of us tend to depreciate experiences in our lives when they happen more than once. The first time I took a trip in an airplane was the most exciting adventure of my whole young life. My second airplane trip was exciting, but not like the first. In the last eight years I've flown so much that fastening my seat belt in a plane is no more exciting than fastening my seat belt in my car. Flying, at least in commercial jetliners, has become perfunctory. We depreciate repeated family experiences in the same way. In fact what may have started out as expressions of love often end up as chores. That's because human love tends to fade as experiences are repeated. But God's love expressed in our family can keep family time together from deteriorating into perfunctory exercises. Dinnertime can be a celebration of love, rather than just a meal. What makes the difference is the expression to each other of the love God has poured out into our hearts. Putting the kids to bed, taking a family walk or a bicycle ride in the park, family devotions, going on a Saturday picnic, painting the front porch together, spending family nights at home can all be precious each time they happen, when we realize that God is working within each family member "both to will and to do His good pleasure" (Philippians 2:13). Whether repeated family functions are perfunctory or precious depends on our investment in them. If all we invest is a certain role, we will function in our families because it's our duty to do so. But if we invest the love of God that has been poured out in our lives, those same functions become precious to us and to our family members.

FOOTNOTES

[1]James Dobson, *Hide or Seek* (Old Tappan, NJ: Fleming H. Revell, 1974), pages 9-13.

7

THE HOLY SPIRIT IN THE CHRISTIAN HOME

". . . the Holy Spirit who was given to us . . ."

A Home Full of Christians	A Christian Home
HAVE RECEIVED THE HOLY SPIRIT	**IS ONE IN THE SPIRIT**
We never walk alone; God lives within us.	Our decision making can be interrelated rather than independent.
God guides our lives from within as well as by His Word.	Family harmony becomes the norm rather than the exception.
God never misunderstands. He sees our lives from our side too.	We listen to our family and to God's Holy Spirit through them.

In the list of results of justification in Romans 5:1-5, the one which makes all the others happen is the last result listed—the Holy Spirit living inside of us. Through the Spirit, God Himself actually lives in us. And the indwelling Holy Spirit is God's personal guarantee that all the results of justification will be ours.

We Never Walk Alone

The implication of this is that every Christian has the assurance that he never walks alone. God lives inside of him—He's actually there. God is not only *out there* in heaven someplace, watching over me, but His Holy Spirit lives *in* me. Knowing that my heavenly Father watches over me gives me the confidence that I am being cared for and protected. But knowing that the Holy Spirit lives within me is even more comforting, because it assures me that He has an empathetic as well as a sympathetic understanding of my life. I understand when my son falls off his bike and skins his elbow. I can see the injury, and I know that it's his elbow hurting. But I'm up here and he's down there, and I feel that it's about time for him to be getting over his crying. But, there may be more to the whole thing than what I see. I see the hurt elbow. I see the cause of physical pain, but I may not notice the injured pride that came along with the fall.

God, our heavenly Father, sees when we fall. He knows our hurts much better than I can possibly know my son's hurts. He's not only aware of injured elbows. He's aware of injured pride, of feelings of inadequacy, frustration and anger. He is also aware of what we think and say inside of ourselves, and of the expletives we repeat softly enough so we won't be heard. It is comforting to know God is that aware.

But the fact that the Holy Spirit lives in me gives

me even more comfort for God sees my falls from my point of view as well as from His. I can't get into my son's life and feel the pain in his elbow. But God has given me His Holy Spirit to live in my life. This enables Him to see not only from above, but from within as well!

Help in Making Decisions

When we talked about Ephesians 5 in the last chapter I pointed out that decision making is not the subject there. The subject is husbands' and wives' relationships with one another after the analogy of Christ and the church. It has to do with self-giving love, not with family decision making. The proper context of decision making for the Christian is the Holy Spirit in our lives. When the Holy Spirit dwells in the life in each person in a family, the result is that the dynamics of decision making are not separate in each person's life. The same Holy Spirit in the wife's life and in the husband's life is leading them each to the same decision. Ideally, there are not two wills involved, but one Will. This is what it means to be one in the Spirit. The Christian family's decision making can be Spirit-led and, therefore, unified. Several passages in Scripture speak of this matter of being led by the Spirit in very definite ways.

The Spirit of Adoption and the Spirit of Slavery

Romans 8:14 shows that being led by the Spirit of God is a telltale sign of the fact that a person is a child of God. This telltale sign is not an identification mark for other Christians or the world to observe. It is a sign of self-identity—a way by which we can know who we are. When I become aware of the Holy Spirit's leading in my life, my identity as a child of God is affirmed.

Verses 15 and 16 contrast the Holy Spirit's leading with a common counterfeit. The spirit of slavery or bondage is often substituted for the "Spirit of adoption." The spirit of slavery is the world's alternative to the Holy Spirit. It is the world's promise of success, wealth, power, popularity, or whatever appeals to you. It becomes a spirit of slavery because it traps you by leaving you unsatisfied and then offering you a little more. You can never get quite enough. Therefore, the spirit of slavery always leads to fear: the fear of losing the success, wealth, power, popularity, and so forth already attained, or the fear that you will never be quite satisfied. In contrast to the spirit of slavery is the spirit of adoption. God adopts us into His family, thereby changing our identity. His Holy Spirit in our lives witnesses to that change of identity by giving us the urge to call God "Daddy, Father."

One of the implications for our families of the fact that the Spirit of God lives in us is that the same Holy Spirit has changed the identities of all the family members who are God's children, and He is affirming their identity as God's children too. As Ephesians 4:4-6 says, "There is one body and one Spirit, just as also you were called in one hope of your calling; one Lord, one Faith, one baptism, one God and Father of all who is over all and through all and in all."

The Rat Maze of Circumstances

How do we make our decisions? Most of us seem to

rely on opening and closing doors to know what God's will is. When I was at UCLA, I took a class on behavioral learning. We were given rats, and each of us was to teach his rat certain kinds of behavior. One of the ways we taught them was to put them through a maze and then open and close various doors. This is the way some of us want God to lead us. We pray, "God if you don't want me to go this way, please close the door in my face." We're asking God to put us into the rat maze and to close and open doors so that we can only go one way, His way.

However, God really wants to lead us in a way that treats us as people, not as rats. He speaks to us personally through convictions in our hearts. If we really believe that God's Holy Spirit lives within us and that He wants to talk with us, then it makes sense to believe that He really does want to guide us personally. This realization will enable us to begin to hear and sense God's will on a regular basis. That's the way that God wants to lead us. In both major decisions and minor decisions God has always chosen to lead His people through His Word and by a still, small voice within. It would be good for us to review this process as it is discussed in 1 Kings 19:9-12, describing how God led Elijah. There must be a harmony between these two sources of guidance. If there is disharmony between them, we shouldn't make a decision. We should wait for more leading.

Consider what Joseph Cooke has said about this:

> Perhaps I can make the issue a little clearer if I attempt to describe two different approaches to the problem of making God-honoring decisions. One approach I call the

direction method, and the other the *wisdom method*.

In the direction method, one tries to make the right decisions by obtaining directions or orders from God. It is assumed that God has something like a blueprint for every Christian—a perfect plan that includes a divinely ordained decision at every turn of the road. The duty of the Christian, then, is to avoid any independent decisions, and at every point to seek and find that perfect plan, that perfect decision from God, and then to do what He says without asking questions, and without any back talk. All decisions should come from headquarters. One should therefore avoid the kind of self-will in which one makes one's own plans, and then tries to sanctify them by adding, "If it be Thy will . . . ." Instead, one should find out God's will before making the decisions, and then act accordingly. It is assumed, furthermore, that God is as eager to communicate His will in any given matter as we are to find it. He may speak to us through Scripture, or through sanctified common sense, or through any one of a wide variety of ways; but, in the final analysis, it is usually necessary to wait for the still small voice of the Holy Spirit giving the final assurance in our hearts. If the voice speaks, all the experience or wisdom in the world should not turn us from the indicated path. If it does not we have no right to move forward.

In the wisdom method, on the other hand, the Christian goes to God for *wisdom* rather than for *direction*. He seeks to know and understand the principles that God lays down in Scripture, prayerfully uses every bit of wisdom God supplies, arrives at the best course of action he can devise, and then acts. This is not to rule out God's direction altogether. God is sovereign, and He can—at any time He chooses—step into our lives and tells us, "Do this!" or, "Do that!" But ordinarily He does not. Even in the more important things such as marriage or vocation, He doesn't give us any very explicit guidance. He merely asks us to do all to the glory of God, and leaves us to determine, under the authority of Scripture, what doing all to the glory of God will mean in any given situation. In other words, in most of the decisions of life, God simply asks us to use our sanctified, biblically informed common sense. This is what I mean by the wisdom method.[1]

We should be thankful when circumstances (open and closed doors) confirm our decisions, and there are times when the issues are so confusing that we can be led by no method but the rat maze one. I don't mind being led by the rat maze method occasionally, but God wants to lead me in a much more intimate way, and I'm missing out on His more personal guidance through the Holy Spirit when I'm only depending on the rat maze. Often, we're just not close enough to hear what God is saying to us. He gave us His Holy Spirit when we were saved so that we would have a far more personal, meaningful, and thrilling means of decision making than the fateful opening and closing of doors.

Growth in Family Harmony

If a family is led by the Holy Spirit within each individual, family harmony becomes the norm rather than the exception. When Evie and I were first married, the reason we didn't have many conflicts was simply because I dominated her. I just overpowered her. I didn't realize what was happening. She so accepted the role of submissiveness and I so accepted the role of leadership that I didn't give her a chance to assert herself at all. That was the reason we didn't have arguments. When I began to realize what I was doing, I began to back off and to try to "nourish and cherish her" (Ephesians 5:29). In some cases I pushed her to make decisions, and she began to assert herself in a healthy way. Then we began to come into conflict periodically. Our next discovery was that when we were both sensitive to God's Holy Spirit and anxious for God to lead us, conflict was very, very rare. On the other hand, when we were ignoring the Holy Spirit and doing our own thing, conflict was inevitable.

We've gotten to the place now that one of the key ways to know whether or not both of us are in tune with the Holy Spirit is to see whether we are in agreement. When we begin to experience a lot of disagreement, we realize that we're not being sensitive to the Holy Spirit. The same Holy Spirit is in both our lives, and He keeps bringing us together. Maybe that sounds idealistic. Maybe it sounds theoretical and "spiritual." But it is very practical and very real to Evie and me.

Someone Really Understands Us

The third implication of the Holy Spirit in our lives is that we have the assurance that we will be understood. God sees life from our side, too. We may misunderstand each other. I often do, but God never misunderstands. When we respond to God's understanding, we listen better to our family. There are fewer misunderstandings between us and we experience the unity of Spirit. Then we don't have to sing "We Are One in the Spirit" wishfully; it becomes a reality.

God gives different people different gifts for two purposes: for building up of the body, and for the work of service. That's true for the family as well as for the church. If we recognize this, we won't be as apt to cop out when difficult decisions have to be made. A wife may cop out by saying, "It's your decision, you're the head of the home." The husband for his part may say, "I delegate this decision to you," and refuse to take responsibility. In a family that is led by the Holy Spirit, we can give each other the gift of the final word.

Evie and I recognize the longer we live together that I'm gifted in some ways that she is not, and she is gifted in other areas where I am not. For instance, she is gifted and I am not in the matter of dressing style. I have poor taste in clothing; her taste is good. My students in the seminary can tell by the way I dress whether my wife got up with me in the morning or whether she slept in. At first it was threatening to me to have my wife say, "Honey, you shouldn't be wearing that tie with that shirt." I thought, "Good grief, am I not mature enough to be able to dress myself?" But she was gentle and kind in the way she told me, so

135

finally, I gave her that gift, concluding that the Holy Spirit placed in her the ability to decide on clothing for both of us. Even when she's not there, I try to ask myself, "What would Evie tell me to wear or not to wear?" I acknowledge her gift in that area, so that she makes our decisions in matters of dress style.

Power to Serve Within Family Roles

You've probably heard about the husband who bragged that he and his wife had divided the decision-making evenly: "I make all the important decisions and my wife makes all the unimportant ones. She makes decisions such as where we're going to live, what school the kids should attend, where I'm going to work, what church we'll join, and so on." His friends asked him, "Good grief, if those are your wife's decisions, what are the important decisions that you make?" His answer was: "How we should handle the Arab oil embargo, what to do about inflation, what the U.S. space program should be like, and so forth."

That little joke indicates the kinds of tensions that arise when we think that because we have a certain role we must make particular kinds of decisions. When the Holy Spirit leads a married couple, He is not limited by role expectations. He will help them make decisions together through whichever partner He has gifted in a certain area. If a married couple adopt this attitude, they will find that they no longer think in terms of "This is a man's decision," "This is a woman's decision." They will say instead, "This is the Holy Spirit's decision, regardless of which channel He used to make it."

The Holy Spirit in the Christian Home

Most of us conform to role expectations because of some kind of fear: fear of failure, fear of reproach, fear that someone will laugh at us, fear of loss of respect. So we act within a role pattern because we've been squeezed into it by the world's mold. Let me suggest that God would have us replace our roles with a quality of life style that is inspired and shaped by the Holy Spirit in both of us. The dominant atmosphere of this life style is service: service to our home, service to our wife or our husband, service to our kids, service to our church and service to the world. We are called to lift the people who cross our path, whoever they are. We are called to lift their self-esteem, to nourish and cherish them. The model for this kind of service is what Jesus did for the church, giving Himself in sacrifice for us.

FOOTNOTES

[1]Joseph Cooke, *Free for the Taking* (Old Tappan, NJ: Fleming H. Revell, 1975), pages 88-89.